PROTESTORS
FOR
PARADISE

PROTESTORS FOR PARADISE

by

FRANCES GUMLEY
AND BRIAN REDHEAD

BBC BOOKS

Published by BBC Books
a division of BBC Enterprises Limited,
Woodlands, 80 Wood Lane, London W12 0TT
First published 1993

ISBN 0 563 36478 5

Designed by Sara Kidd

Set in 11/14pt Stempel Garamond by Redwood Press Ltd, Melksham
Printed and bound in Great Britain by Redwood Press Ltd, Melksham
Jacket printed by Lawrence Allen, Weston-super-Mare

CONTENTS

INTRODUCTION

This book began life as a radio series for BBC Radio 4, presented by Brian Redhead, scripted by Frances Gumley and produced by Malcolm Love. The series and now this book explore the phenomenon of Christian conflict which has bedeviled and inspired the Church throughout its life.

It recognises that for many priests, teachers, believers and preachers, protest has been the only way of expressing their faith. In the company of eminent scholars, a few clerics, a statistician and a cleaner, *Protestors for Paradise* asks what is behind this hunger for reform. Is it a sign of strength, or a symptom of a message so compromised that in all honesty it should be abandoned?

If you have ever wondered why so many Christians, from Savonarola to Hans Küng, have spent their lives attacking their fellow Christians and, if not biting, at least trying to change the Church which formed them, join us in this book on the trail of the Protestors for Paradise in search of reforms ancient, modern and yet to come.

*Francis of Assisi receiving a papal blessing. Later Franciscans like
William of Ockham would find the strict allegiance to the Franciscan
ideal of poverty would bring them into confrontation with Rome.*

CHAPTER I

RANTERS AND RAZORS

'We must now combat and dispute against heretics who are plunged into a thousand errors. Their doctrine does not come from God as their lives, soiled and blackened by sin, clearly show.'

Savonarola: Triumph of the Cross

'The hell hound of Rome, not the Turk, is the true enemy of Christianity.'
'Mad dog!'
'Boar!'
'Fox!'

The words of Christians not at prayer, but in protest

Throughout its history the Christian Church has been as well known for its disputes as for its dogmas, but in the centuries which marked the end of the Middle Ages the pace of protest intensified as never before until a tide of reforms built up which would overwhelm and change for ever both the Church and the world into which the reformers had been born.

Theirs is a story of idealism and treachery, of power, politics and gory martyrdoms, of blind bigotry and courageous goodness. The reformers, a mixed bag if ever there was one, looked beyond this world. They were campaigners for today and tomorrow. They were agitators for more than this world. They were protestors for paradise and they are still among us now.

To understand their reforms, which are still unfinished, it is essential to forget twentieth century ecclesiastical labels and to look beyond the pulpit and the parish. The Reformation was and is no single event. In this book, we pursue it back to the thirteenth century and forwards to the twenty-first. In the chase, theology will be important but so too will be social change, disease, the impetus of new inventions, and the unpredictable nature of individual men and women.

But first let us discard unwanted fish. To think of religion as the specialised pursuit of the pious is a twentieth-century red herring. In twentieth century terms, as Dr Eamon Duffy of Magdalene College, Cambridge, explains, religion is, in a sense, a leisure time occupation and when we talk about religion we often mean simply people's beliefs and convictions – what is going on inside their heads.

But religion had a much wider and more inclusive meaning in the late Middle Ages and the early modern period. People used religion to structure their whole world. To take the example of the parish Mass on Sunday, people went – obviously – to worship God and, in particular, to worship Christ, whom they believed was brought into the church and onto the altar by the words of consecration. But they also went to church to express their sense of community solidarity. Many of the ceremonies of the Mass are social rituals. For example, the parish procession which preceded every Sunday Mass was an event in which people walked in order of seniority within the parish; taking part in that procession was the way of establishing your place in the social pecking order. For us that may seem to be a secular function, but medieval Christians thought of religion as giving form and meaning to life, including social life. Establishing order and precedence, harmony and peace within the secular community was a religious activity. So, where as we would now see going to communion as an act of personal religion linking us directly to God, they saw it as plugging into a social harmony which was the life of God in the world.

However, that harmony was under attack. The growth of towns and commerce and the subtle shift from regional to national identities showed that change was possible. The Church could no longer expect to rule unquestioned. Secular kings and princes began to resent the idea that their jurisdiction fell short of the clergy. At the end of the thirteenth century Pope Celestine V, the semi-literate hermit pope who had retained a taste for extreme austerity and fruity peasant invective, resigned the See of Rome. Previously unshakeable precedents could now clearly be broken. In England the Bible began to be translated into accessible everyday language. John Wyclif, the English philosopher and reformer, questioned the need for priests and was condemned by Rome. His followers, known as Lollards, continued preaching after his death. His ideas reached as far as Prague where they influenced Jan Hus, the rector of the university there who was to become one of the earliest martyrs of the Reformation.

England, Czechoslovakia – what linked the reformers other than historical coincidence? Gordon Leff, Professor Emeritus of York University, believes that what they all had in common was the conviction that you should look to the Bible for true doctrine and the true example of Christ, and that if you do, what you find there is very different from the doctrine which had been developed in the Church. Canon Law, in particular, was one of the great phobias of reformers. Dante had much to say against it, both in the *Divine Comedy* and in his book on monarchy. The other constant theme was the flagrant contradiction and incompatibility between the Church as a privileged institution with a full range of temporal powers, including the ability to employ coercive power, and Christ's own life as a simple, homeless and possessionless wanderer, who took nothing for the morrow. His kingdom was not of this world, and He employed no forms of judgement at all, but simply preached spiritual reformation through belief in Him.

Of course Francis of Assisi, the little man who was the friend of Brother Wolf and of Brother Fire, had preached the same return to the simplicity of the Gospels. What turned a reformer into a protestant was questioning the authority of the Pope – that is where the frontline battles of the Reformation would be fought. But Bernard Hamilton, Professor of Crusading History at Nottingham University, says it is wrong to think that other religious ideas were not being questioned.

He maintains that there is a lot of good evidence (for instance in the records of the Inquisition) that there was a certain degree of scepticism about individual items of the faith, although they were not necessarily those over which the reformers would have disagreed with the Pope. An instance of this, and a matter which was subject to very considerable doubt in the Middle Ages, was belief in the resurrection of the body. A body can be seen to decompose, in which case the doctrine of resurrection simply appears to go against common sense. There was also fairly widespread scepticism about the virgin birth, although this was not something which was a matter of contention between Catholic and Protestant in the sixteenth century: both accepted it as scriptural truth.

These ideas and doubts were spread all over Europe. They did not begin in Luther's Germany or in Henry VIII's England. Reform respected no geographical, social or sectarian boundaries. To prove this point we call three witnesses; a thin-faced ascetic Englishman, a fiery unbalanced Italian and a genial Dutch gentleman who loved good company and loathed English beer.

First of all, the Englishman – William of Ockham, Franciscan and philosopher. He observed: 'In argument, when you can do with less, do not posit more.'

This piece of common sense came to be known as 'Ockham's Razor'. It is hardly the stuff of revolution. But William, born at the end of the thirteenth century, lived at a time when elaborate repetitious proofs of the existence of God were the philosophical and theological vogue – the scholastic way. William hit at the heart of accepted theology. Marilyn Adams, Professor of Philosophy at the University of California, explains that unlike many of his medieval predecessors, Ockham rejected the idea that any of the liturgical or sacramental acts caused changes in the soul. He wanted to regard sacramental acts or liturgy simply as occasions on which God had promised to produce salvific changes. Thus there was no causal connection between the bread and wine of the Eucharist on the one hand, and the changes in the soul or its soteriological status on the other. In this denial of any kind of efficient causal connection between liturgy and the sacramental acts, and changes in the status of the soul, Ockham anticipated a number of different themes which were to recur in the Reformation.

The Church supervised the sacraments. William the academic was merely being logical but he was seen as undermining the power of the Church over the souls of its adherents. Worse was to come. William observed that faith was faith and could not be proved. He questioned the need for intermediary forms or ideas either in philosophy or in theology. And then the quiet friar from Surrey began to protest in earnest.

Gordon Leff says that in the second half of William's career he became a rebel with other members of this Franciscan order, who refused to accept the Pope's decree concerning the observation of certain Franciscan practices of poverty. William then turned the same solvent – so to speak – against the Church. He said that it was possible, in fact, to have a Church without a Pope. God could have disposed of matters entirely differently. But, equally, if He had wished it, He could have said that you could do without the hierarchy entirely and, instead, have a single individual standing for the Church in this world. All of this helped to cast doubt on the irremovability of time-honoured institutions, and that is where he joined forces with all those other people, all the way to Luther himself.

William was in serious trouble. He had been summoned to Avignon in 1324 to answer charges of philosophical heresy but now his attack on Church structures meant that reconciliation was impossible. William took to his feet. He fled from Avignon in 1327 with the leader of his order. William joined Emperor Ludwig of Bavaria who was engaged in a war – mainly of words – with the Pope, because of the Pope's refusal to recognise his claim to become the new Emperor. William became what is called a publicist, or a campaigning journalist. He started to write treatises, often polemics, against what he regarded as the pretensions of absolute papal power, and the abuses of papal authority.

This second phase of William's career, says Gordon Leff, was much more immediately influential because it had a considerable bearing on the theories which helped to form what is called the concilliar movement – the period from 1376 to 1417 of great councils of the Church which tried to overcome the divisions at first between two Popes, later three, when each of them laid claims to universality. Ockham's doctrines were certainly important there.

William found himself cast in the role of revolutionary. In spite of all his harsh criticism of individual Popes, William was not anti-papal. He wanted reform not revolution. Marilyn Adams thinks that one reason why people are quick to connect Ockham as a precursor of the Reformation is that he was a very vigorous critic of the papacy, and of Pope John XXII in particular. He argued, and applied certain theories in Canon Law to argue, that John XXII, in contradicting the pronouncements of earlier Popes on Franciscan poverty, had thereby become a publically proclaimed heretic – and no true Pope. Ockham pressed this charge enthusiastically in public debate and this is why he is connected, by many, with the Reformation. There was, however, one major difference between Ockham and the later reformers. Ockham did not reject the office of the papacy itself; he thought that Christ had freely and contingently stipulated that the Church was to be ruled by a monarch. The papacy, therefore, was Christ's will and his criticism was not of the office itself but of the incumbent who, in his view, was no true incumbent.

Perhaps also Ockham anticipated some later views; for example, that papal government should be much like secular government. He had a minimalist conception of the papacy, believing that papal government of the Church should be conditioned by the ideal of evangelical liberty, just as secular government should be conditioned by the ideal of individual liberty. In his view, therefore, the pope should not lay down rules and regulations for their own sake, but only those that were necessary. Once again, while Ockham was a vigorous critic of the pope, he was not in favour of abolishing the office itself.

There was no immediate successor to William, not because of any ecclesiastical reason but, as Gordon Leff believes, because of something even deadlier. Like so many of his generation – the generation which preceded the Black Death – William marked a watershed, because the Black Death carried off so many of his contemporaries. There was really a hiatus of twenty years or so before the resumption of real intellectual activity in the 1360s. There is no doubt at all that reformers like Luther were very aware of Ockham, because he was the head of what was then called the Nominalist School.

William died quietly in Munich around 1349. The Franciscan grave-yard where he was buried is now a car park but it has a small plaque in his memory. William was a rigorous thinker but no firebrand.

Our second witness, the Italian Girolamo Savonarola, who was born about 100 years after William's death, could not have been more different. A man not given to mincing his words, his view of those who held different religious views was clear if not conciliatory. He stated: 'He never errs who observes the Christian faith. All other beliefs are execrable.'

There have been many differing opinions about Savonarola, the mesmeric preacher and prophet who for a few years held Florence in his thrall. He was put to the stake when his anti-papal statements placed his city in danger. Before and after that event he was regarded by some as a saint. A fiercely unbending Catholic, he was hailed by some early Protestants as a reforming hero. What sort of a human being lies behind such conflicting reputations?

Eamon Duffy says that nowadays we would categorise Savonarola as a religious fanatic. He was an extreme puritan. He preached religious revival in Florence and converted hundreds of the citizens. Some of the results were disastrous in terms of the history of culture. He organised the famous Bonfires of the Vanities, when he called on Florentines to burn rich clothing and ornaments. Botticelli, the painter, was converted

HIERONYMI·FERRARIENSIS·A·DEO·
≈·MISSI·PROPHETÆ·EFFIGIES·≈

*Girolamo Savonarola, a fiercely unbending Catholic
with a penchant for bonfires, who was hailed as both a
traditionalist bigot and as a reforming hero*

by Savonarola and burned many of his masterpieces. After his conversion, he did not paint any more pagan pictures like the famous *Primavera* but produced rather stiff and forbidding religious compositions instead.

Savonarola was a visionary figure; he had tremendously high ideals and he was one of the greatest preachers of the fifteenth century – a century which was unusually rich in great preachers, many of them hot gospel revivalist preachers in the Billy Graham mould, as indeed was Savonarola. He was a giant, but he must have been rather daunting and uncomfortable to live with.

John Bossy, Professor of History at York University, believes that hearing Savonarola in full spate would have been an unforgettable experience. He preached in the Duemo, the cathedral of Florence, a fairly new building at that time – its dome had only been added about 50 years before. One can imagine the scene: a vast space with few interruptions, rather modern in that sense, with almost nothing between him and his audience.

He was preaching at a time when people were very conscious of the four last things: death, judgement, heaven and hell. He would normally preach a series of sermons in Lent, when people were being advised to think about their souls, about penance and about going to confession to pour out their sins. He set out to convince his listeners that they were sinners, and to explain the ways in which they were sinful. Added to that, he hammered home a very simple message: if they went on being sinful, dreadful things would happen to them personally and to the world at large.

At one level, he was a fire-and-brimstone preacher, but he had a speciality. His particular line was to say that if his listeners continued to indulge in sodomy, usury, murder or whatever else they happened to be doing, not only would they roast in hell for all eternity, but some frightful disaster would happen – here and now. It might be the bubonic plague or something else, but whatever it was, it was certain to be deeply unpleasant.

On one occasion, Savonarola prophesied the coming of an avenging army, over the Alps. It would sack the city and, in the process, do God's work by punishing sin. This was amazingly specific, and it just so happened that it all came about, as he had predicted. A French army did arrive, in huge force, a little more than a year after he had prophesied it and, naturally, this gave him an instant reputation of being an infallible oracle. He was the man with a direct line to God. It was after this that one of his contemporaries commented that when you listened to Savonarola, your hair stood on end. In part, this was due to the feeling that here was a man with immediate knowledge of divine vengeance; in part, also, it was a reaction to Savonarola's extraordinary and highly individual way of preaching.

He preached in a sort of howl or moan, and you can get some idea of this from reading his sermons. He is always declaiming 'Oh this' or 'Oh that' and, with a little effort, you can imagine these howls, moans and cries echoing round and round the church. It must have, quite literally, put the fear of God into people.

But Savonarola achieved more than this. Not only did he put the fear of God into his listeners; he also brought them legal, social and tax reforms. For a few years, worldly Florence became a puritan enclave. In the Bonfire of the Vanities, he persuaded people to burn their make up, their jewellery, their wigs and pornographic books. He even left his mark on art. Vasari, the Italian art historian, in his *Lives of the Painters*, describes how Botticelli eventually turned his back on art because of his ardent support for Savonarola's teachings. It is also possible that Savonarola's bonfires might hold the clue to a conundrum of the fine art world.

Dr Patricia Morrison, art critic of the *Financial Times*, says that the two Bonfires of the Vanities held in two successive years, must have been an extraordinary, fantastic spectacle. For the first one, a type of wooden pyramid was erected. It was 60 feet high and must have looked rather like the spire of a gothic cathedral. This pyramid had niches all the way up its sides, and in these niches the faithful were encouraged to put their objects of vanity – things that were going to make their lives more pleasant, but which might also distract a man or woman from giving sufficient thought to the state of their soul.

So the Florentines brought out their chess boards, lutes and other musical instruments, portrait busts and paintings, and the entire lot was committed to the flames. It has been pointed out that there are very few Botticelli nudes still in existence, although it is known that in the early stages of his career he was famous for them. They were commissioned pieces for the well-to-do, who displayed them in the privacy of their houses. Why should there only be two left? Could it be, perhaps, that most of them went up in smoke?

There is a limit, however, to the amount of good – and in particular of repentance – that people can stand. Inevitably, Savonarola crossed swords with the vastly corrupt Borgia Pope, Alexander VI. Alexander, said Savonarola, was an anti-christ, proof that the Church and the papacy needed reform. The Pope responded by excommunicating Savonarola and, for good measure, he put the city of Florence under interdict as well. Savonarola's days were numbered. The people of Florence constructed a pyre, suspended Savonarola's body over it, and crowded round to watch their former guardian die.

The city's mood had been changed by Savonarola's campaign against the Pope. But how could a Pope as immoral as Alexander VI command any respect at all? Michael Walsh, Librarian of Heythrop College, London, says that to understand how someone like Alexander could be tolerated it must be remembered that our image of the papacy is largely based on the way the papacy has developed over the last 150 years. In the Middle Ages, the papacy's image was rather different.

People were, of course, a little shocked by Alexander who was, to put it kindly, one of the more unusual Popes. He fathered ten children (all of them, by definition, illegitimate), and no pope, before or since, has left a daughter in charge of the Vatican and married sundry other children in the Vatican Palace. So he, and to a lesser extent some of his successors, must be seen as Renaissance princes first and foremost, overwhelmingly concerned with their own – and their dynastic – ambitions. They were not spiritual leaders in the modern sense of the term.

At one point, when one of his children was murdered and dumped in the Tiber, Alexander had a change of heart and set up a commission to investigate church reform. But it came to nothing and Alexander's personal reform was fleeting.

There was laxity not only in Rome. A sizeable minority of the supposedly celibate priesthood were married in all but name. This brings us to the last of our three witnesses – the genial Dutchman, Erasmus of Rotterdam, satirist and scholar who wrote: 'Monks – the whole tribe is now so universally loathed that even a chance meeting is thought to be ill omened, yet they are gloriously self-satisfied. They believe that it is the highest form of piety to be so uneducated that they cannot even read. They bray like donkeys in church, repeating by rote the psalms they have not understood.'

Behind that invective was one of the best brains of his age – and a man with an unusual background. Michael Smith, a church historian and Baptist minister from Golcar in Yorkshire, points out that Erasmus had a

Erasmus of Rotterdam, arguably the best brain of his age, a brilliant satirist who inspired reform and loathed English beer

very strange upbringing. If you were to apply modern psychological theory, he had every excuse for being thoroughly bitter and twisted.

He was the illegitimate son of a priest in the Netherlands and was brought up in his early years in a rather strict and pious school. Orphaned by the age of twelve, he was propelled into a monastery which he heartily detested. Eventually, he managed to work his way out of it, by becoming a bishop's secretary. However, he had another string to his bow.

From his earliest days he had a great love of classical literature. He started with the Latin classics and then went on – partly at the instance of John Colet, the Dean of St. Paul's – to turn his mind to the scriptures. This involved him in learning, and becoming highly proficient in, Greek. He edited some of the Greek Fathers and then produced his edition of the Greek New Testament which burst like a bombshell into the literary and religious world of 1516. Right through to the end of his life, he was the best mind of his day – so much so that later, after Luther had surfaced and Christendom was split, both sides tried to wheedle Erasmus into identifying with their own camps. Such was his prestige. When you read about other people in other places, his name comes up, again and again, as the source of their inspiration, either direct or at second-hand. He wrote and travelled extensively, he knew a huge number of people and was a key figure in the period when the Reformation began.

Individual brilliance, however, is enough to spark off but not to sustain charge. Part of the reason why the work of the early reformers failed to have a lasting impact lay not in theology or in politics but in the mechanics of book production. Professor Bernard Hamilton argues that, to understand the Church before the Reformation, you need to think yourself back into a society in which literacy was a minority accomplishment. Even in places like Florence in the fifteenth century no more than a quarter of the adult male population would have been able to read and write, and Florence was fairly exceptional. In addition, before the invention of printing, book production was immensely expensive. There is a story about St. Francis of Assisi which illustrates this.

One day, an old woman came to the Friary at Assisi and asked for help. The brothers had nothing to give her, so they told Francis about her. He said 'You must have something to give her,' but they told him they had nothing at all apart from the clothes they stood in. But they did have one other possession: a copy of the New Testament which they used for reading lessons in chapel. St. Francis said, 'Give it to her.' Now if you were to give a hungry old woman a copy of the New Testament today, you would probably get little thanks for it. But the old woman in the story was not expected to be able to read the New Testamant, and it was not given to her in the hope that she would. What she could do was sell it and live on the proceeds.

Since books cost so much to produce, the idea of making them generally accessible was something of a non-starter. At best, a book might reach a larger audience if it was read aloud. Printing was invented during the course of the fifteenth century but it only really took off towards the century's close. Even then, books were pretty expensive. Nevertheless, there was for the first time the potential for disseminating new ideas on a previously unimaginable scale.

The genius of Erasmus has never been in question. He knew the Church was crying out for reform. His way of calling for change was to poke fun at its weaknesses, most famously in *Praise Of Folly*, dashed off during a stay with Thomas More in London. He was no leader of a popular movement but rather the foremost thinker in a pan-European circle of the literary elite, the humanists – a misleading title, Professor Cornelius Augustijn of Amsterdam University believes.

He points out that a humanist in the world of 1500 was not an agnostic or an atheist but a Christian who studied classical antiquity and was steeped in Greek and Latin literature. This was not done purely out of antiquarian zeal. There was an ideal behind the study, and a belief that you could become more complete as a person through studying these authors. That was Erasmus' conviction, and *Praise of Folly* shows this. The entire book is a marvellous game, with all manner of quotations and allusions from antiquity, just the sort of book that Christian humanists in the Europe of 1500 revelled in. So to call someone a Christian humanist implied more than mere affection for the ancient world. It was not simply a matter of looking back to an idealised past. It had implications for reform. Michael Smith points out that a humanist was a follower of the new learning as opposed to the rather arid philosophising of the scholars of the Middle Ages. It was a departure, also, from the all-embracing ignorance of many of the higher clergy, some of whom were unable even to sign their own names.

Humanists also tended to be somewhat subversive, since they asked awkward questions about many of the current traditions. One of Erasmus' great heroes was an Italian humanist who committed the cardinal sin of questioning the authorship of the Apostles' Creed – according to a myth which was in vogue at the time, each of the Apostles was supposed to have contributed one phrase.

Also, it was the humanists who urged a return to the best available ancient text in order to outflank subsequent medieval accretions, and this made them awkward bedfellows with that largest and most pervasive of medieval multinationals, the Church of Rome.

Erasmus had no illusions about the Church in which he had grown up, but he was a critic rather than a rebel. He hoped for reform from within, and he was saddened when such reform did not materialise. He was terribly disillusioned when, on his first visit to Italy, he saw the Pope entering Bologna as a victorious general. In fact, such was his distaste for what he had seen that he composed a rather nasty little tract called (after the offending Pope): *Julius Excluded from the Heavens*. He was, however, deeply dismayed by the divisions which came later, and urged a meeting of good, honourable, godly men from all traditions to see whether matters could be sorted out and, perhaps, a few differences tolerated.

But the time for toleration and compromise was running out. The first half of the sixteenth century would see the Church of Ockham, Savonarola and Erasmus convulsed. In their own ways, the Englishman, the Italian and the Dutchman had helped to make reform inevitable.

William, the quiet friar from Surrey, is remembered more by philosophers than by historians of the Church. He deserves more from the Church. As Marilyn Adams says, Ockham had a radical ideal of what the Church could be. He believed that Christ had declared that the Church, like the state, should be ruled by a monarch. But in the case of the Church, the monarch's role should be pastoral rather than temporal. William wanted a Church whose members would enjoy freedom of thought; where those in power would only legislate when necessary, and whose members would be free to pursue their way to salvation as they saw fit. Ockham was very much against the legalistic Church, in which all the requirements of evangelical perfection would be legislated for. In his view, such a course would only make the law of Christ even more burdensome than the law of Moses, and he did not shrink from saying so. He was an idealist who sacrificed everything in order to defend the Franciscan ideal of poverty, and all his intellectual powers were devoted to its defence.

Giralomo Savonarola, the hellfire-and-brimstone preacher, might seem to be the least sympathetic of our trio. But his very ferocity as a preacher was a reaction to the corruption he saw about him. In Florence, he caught and led the spirit of his age for a time.

To understand his appeal, you have to understand his world. As Eamon Duffy says, in the fifteenth and sixteenth centuries, people lived with an intensity which would now seem utterly alien. Their lives were often short. They lived on the edge of eternity. This was the age of the great urban epidemics, so periodic calls to repent, to remember death and to abandon worldly vanities were fascinating and compelling. They lived hectic lives and their praying was imbued with a comparable sense of feverish urgency. We now tend to think of religious activity as being cool, calm and collected, but in the fifteenth and sixteenth centuries it often took rather exaggerated forms, calling people from a fierce attachment to, and enjoyment of, the things of this world to an unworldly meditation on death and the hereafter – and people felt this tug very strongly.

In Italian culture, too, there is the contrast between carnival on the one hand – often riotous and rather dissolute – and Lent on the other, which was rather severe – no meat or, on most days, eggs or cheese either, which made for a somewhat austere diet. That contrast between ferocious enjoyment and ferocious religion is woven into the period, and Savonarola was very much a part of it. Desiderius Erasmus knew no such extremes, but his impact was even greater. It was said that he laid the egg which an Augustinian canon called Luther would hatch.

As Professor Augustijn points out, there could not have been a Luther without a broad movement towards change among many people – change in society, certainly, but also in the Church and theology. They were not afraid to criticise the Church and those who held power within it. Erasmus belonged to that movement and was the most outstanding figure within it. In a sense, then, the Reformation started with him.

Martin Luther as a young Augustinian friar and loyal son of the Catholic Church, noted for his scholarship, his preaching, his intensity and his calm authority

CHAPTER II

THE MAVERICK MONK

'A leper and a loathsome fellow ... a false libeller and calumniator ... a dog and the son of a bitch, born to snap and bite at the sky with his canine mouth ... having a brain of brass and a nose of iron.'

The considered opinion of Rome concerning a young German theologian called Martin Luther who would change the religious landscape of his world forever.

'Antichrist is enthroned in God's very temple. Farewell you unhappy, lost and blasphemous Rome. The anger of God has come upon you at last.'

The verdict of Martin Luther (1483–1546), former Augustinian friar, on the Pope, the papal court and a Church apparently deaf to the cries for reform which had been gaining strength right across Europe.

Rome, in the shape of the gold-monocled Leo X, a man who was fond of carnivals and hunting, completely misjudged the impact of Luther as a teacher and more significantly failed to grasp the implications of a new form of technology. This is the failure, as much as any corruption and theological backwoodsmanship, which a divided Christendom is still paying for today.

Luther was not a lone voice. The Church was seen to be rich and yet she levied taxes. That has never been a recipe for popularity, but these problems were not new. This chapter uncovers why Luther succeeded where so many others had failed. Before his 95 theses gained him condemnation from Rome, was there anything which marked him out from the earlier reformers? Was there anything exceptional in his background? Dr Ian Siggins, who has made a special study of the women in Luther's life says that Luther used to delight in telling his students that he was a peasant, the son of a peasant and the grandson of a peasant which, in a literal sense, was true. His father and grandfather came from relatively well-to-do peasantry although Hans Luther – Martin Luther's father – had not inherited the family farm. So he had to choose between living in rural poverty and getting an occupation elsewhere. He chose the latter, opting for the growth industry of Thuringia – the silver mines.

While he was embarking on a career in the silver mining industry, he married into the middle class. His wife, Margaret, came from a respected and highly educated family called Lindemann who lived in the nearby market town of Eisenach. Previous generations of her family had been university graduates, magistrates, teachers and doctors. On his mother's side, therefore, Martin Luther was born into a rather substantial and respected family.

When he wanted to, Luther could draw on his father's peasant roots. He could be bawdy and earthy. He was also intellectually brilliant and was given every encouragement by his parents to excel. Hans and Margaret were socially ambitious on Martin's behalf and made sure he went to the well-to-do Lindemanns in Eisenach to complete his schooling.

This was to have more than just an academic effect. The young Martin Luther found himself in an intensely religious household. His aunt and his uncle were much influenced by the local Franciscans who were fiery, austere preachers and, in their own way, reformers. After completing his school studies, Luther read law at the University of Leipzig, but law was not to be his vocation.

According to pious tradition, Luther decided on a religious life during a thunderstorm. However strong the storm, it is far more likely that his religious commitment had been brewing from the childhood days spent in the hot-house piety of his aunt and uncle's house. He joined the Augustinians and began to study theology. His order soon recognised they were dealing with an exceptional young man.

According to John Todd, publisher and biographer of Luther, the Augustinians sent Luther off to the recently founded University of Wittenberg to be the new leading light there. He did his doctorate and became a Professor of Bible Studies. Then, one day, he stood in for the local parish priest and delivered the sermon, and everyone was most impressed. He became the most talked about young man in Wittenberg. The young Luther was quietly memorable. He had an intense voice, flashing eyes and an insistent, charismatic way of preaching, so far as can be made out. He did not shout or bluster as was his way in his later writings; he spoke with calm authority.

The intense young monk was destined for greater fame. He became infuriated by one particular money-making venture – the sale of indulgences. The idea behind indulgences was that it was possible, by certain deeds or prayers performed in this life, to shorten the punishment for sin in the next. So far, so good. However, the next refinement turned indulgences into a shameful scandal. Fund-raising preachers did the rounds voicing terrifying sermons about the punishments in the after-life and then offering indulgences for sale. In other words, they were teaching that money could buy you a ticket for heaven.

Martin Luther was incensed. He fired off his 95 theses in protest to the local archbishop. These are now seen as the trumpet call which heralded 'The Reformation' proper. Such a view misreads Luther. He wanted to remove the taint of racketeering from the theology of indulgences.

The image of a rebel nailing his challenge to Rome on the door of Wittenberg's Castle Church owes more to romance than to attested history. Patrick Collinson, Regius Professor of Modern History at Cambridge, says that there is no really reliable record until after his death of his nailing the theses to the door. There are those who think it never happened, and that all he did was to send them off, very obediently and properly, to his father in God, Archbishop Albrecht of Mainz, saying that he had a few difficulties and would be happy if the Archbishop would sort them out – implying he was sure that this indulgence scandal was going on without the Archbishop's authority.

In fact he was being disingenuous. It was all part of the holy poker game. He knew perfectly well what he was doing, and it was a protest. Whether or not he actually nailed the theses to the door, he was still announcing a university debate on matters which, in his view, were at the very heart of the Christian religion. What happened next was genuinely unexpected, as far as he was concerned. The theses were copied and printed, and despatched to other parts of Germany. He found that he had lit the fuse to a very big powder keg.

Helped by new technology, Luther's theses gained a momentum he could never have predicted. John Todd believes the nailing of the theses is a side issue. What made them notorious was the fact that he involved the local Archbishop. He waited for Albrecht to reply to his letter of complaint. After about a fortnight, he decided to show the theses to one or two of his friends, and then it all started. The friends saw how apt they were, and they were sent to the local printer in town after town. Luther was playing for very high stakes, but politically he was naïve. He had no idea that there would be this tremendous and rather frightening response to his letter to the Archbishop, and he had no idea that the letter would automatically set wheels turning in Rome.

The Archbishop was vaguely irritated, and he knew that if he sent this complaint to Rome, measures would be taken to stop the bleatings of this tiresome young friar in the outer reaches of Christendom. But in the meantime there was this enormous response, with everyone talking about Luther and his theses. Within a year, Erasmus' publisher, Froben, wrote to Luther asking if he could print some of his work. Luther obligingly sent off some material; his desk was always crammed with freshly written papers. The theses were simply the latest outpourings in his preparations for lectures.

Froben liked what he saw, and said he wanted to offer it for sale at the next Frankfurt bookfair. Luther readily agreed, but Froben took great care not to print his own name on the book, and the man who wrote the introduction – and a very excited bit of writing it is too – also took great care not to print his own name. Both of them knew that this topic could lead to the stake, if it were shown to be heretical.

Albrecht was extremely angry, because he had a vested interest in the sale of indulgences; apart from anything else, he relied on a fifty per cent share of the takings to pay his debts. Luther had no idea of the implications of his simple, honest indignation.

Luther had already gained a reputation for strong mindedness which was just as well. He was to need all his certainty, because now, thanks to the printing press, there could be no turning back. Rome called on Luther to recant; he refused. Pope Leo summoned him to Rome. Luther refused to go and denied the primacy of the office of pope for good measure. Luther's original theses had been a call for academic debate. So what was the secret of his success among people *outside* the academic world? Dr Bob Scribner, British Academy Research Reader at Cambridge, says that Luther brought a different message about salvation, telling people that it was more direct and much easier to achieve than they had been led to believe. He also said that salvation was free and that there was no need to pay for religious services. Moreover, he told people that, if they had a good relationship with God, everything would go well.

There is a rather engaging story about a Polish diplomat who visited Luther in 1522 and, on the way, heard peasants complaining that it was Luther's fault that their crops were spoiled due to his opposition to the Pope. There was a reverse side to this. Preachers were going round saying that, since Luther was a godly and virtuous man, people would receive God's blessing if they took up his ideas. To a certain extent, then, Luther was seen as a prophet or holy man; a man who understood the Bible, was pious and spoke the truth. There was also the idea that the end of the world was imminent, and that Luther was exposing false teaching before the last great battle with the antichrist. And, of course, the prospect of imminent annihilation helps to concentrate the mind wonderfully.

Luther expanded his teaching. Faith in Jesus as the Son of God would bring the believer to God. Grace was available through the Word of God. Men and women did not save themselves but God saved them by grace. Luther's teaching was grounded in orthodoxy. John Todd points out that all Luther's really inspiring theology was learned during his early years in the priory, reciting the office with his brethren, studying the Bible and puzzling over it. He was in line with all other people who struggled through to what today one might call an existential response to the Bible, asking what does it really mean for our world. Luther was stretching beyond the whole formula of how you should respond to the Bible. He was struggling to get beyond the scholastic stalemate. In an early lecture, he says – according to notes taken down by a student – 'Oh it is a great thing to be a Christian man and have a hidden life, hidden not in some cell like the hermits, or even in the human heart, which is an unsearchable abyss, but in the invisible God himself, and so to live in the things of the world, but to feed on Him who never appears except in the one vehicle of the hearing of the word.'

In that you can hear late medieval man; you can hear Rhineland mysticism and Luther's own very personal experience, which was going to flower eventually into a full-blown theology of justification by faith.

There was much about Luther which was new and liberating, but in other ways he remained a conventional late medieval cleric. For instance, his views on marriage were hardly radical. Patrick Collinson says Luther thought that marriage was, in some sense, evil but then he also believed that everything in this earth was evil, and since priests were no different from other people they had to be mixed up in the unsatisfactory nature of things. He wrote some amazingly down-to-earth observations about marriage. He spoke about how difficult it is to get on with your wife or your husband, and how there is a great deal of slave labour, and how you could be washing nappies in the middle of the night – he speaks in those terms – and yet he says if you do it in faith, and if you know the meaning of what you are doing, then everything which is outwardly bitter becomes sweet. Luther's talk could be very chauvinistic in present day terms, although that was probably the norm at the time. For instance, he once said that women had large buttocks and that, therefore, it was only right and proper that they should use them for sitting on, at home.

Luther's attitude to woman and to marriage was to change dramatically after his marriage to the former nun, Katherine von Bora. Ian Siggins says that even before his marriage, Luther's chauvinism had not been complete. He had already written one of his most beautifully affective works on the Magnificat, in which the more feminine side of his character was richly expressed. In spite of what some of the textbooks say, he said many wonderful things about the Virgin Mary – for instance that she has no equal amongst humankind. But so far as lesser females were concerned, there is no doubt at all that his marriage to Katie was a surprise. He actually said to a friend of his, just after his marriage, 'I am not in love, nor do I burn with desire, but I cherish my wife as God wished.'

A year later, however, he was talking quite differently. He said that the first year of marriage is one of strange sensations; you are sitting at the table and suddenly you think, 'Before, I was alone, but now there are two of us, and in bed you wake up and see a pair of plaits lying beside you.' He also remarked on the way in which wives can happily pour out all sorts of rather pointless comments, as when Katie suddenly asked him – when he happened to be studying hard – 'Lord Doctor, is the Hochmeister the Margrave's brother?'

Luther said that the highest grace of God is when love flowers perpetually in marriage, and after his marriage he talked in a far more human way. In the rest of his writings also, it is possible to see the way in which becoming a husband, father and family man started to affect even the way in which he thought about good and evil.

By this time Luther was excommunicated. He had been an outlaw and, during the time he was laying low, had translated the New Testament into German to make it available directly to all those who could read. The

Katherine von Bora, the ex-nun who changed Luther's mind about women and marriage

work of translation had always prompted some of Luther's finest insights, even while he was still a monk. John Todd cites in particular the early part of the Gospels where you have John the Baptist and Jesus saying 'repent'. In Latin this is translated as 'do penance', and that was all most people had ever read. Therefore the gospel brought to their minds an image of priest and penitent in the confessional, but in fact the Greek word is 'metanoia', which means a change of heart or a change of mind, and this realisation was a marvellous illumination of Luther's mind.

At about this time, when he had seen this meaning, he described how his spiritual superior wrote to him advising him to turn away from himself to the love of God. He wrote this letter about two years later:

Those words 'the love of God' stuck in me like some sharp and mighty arrow, and I began from that time onward to look up what the scriptures teach about penitence, and then what a game began; the words came up to me on every side, jostling one another and smiling in agreement, so that where before there was hardly any word in the whole of scripture more bitter to me than 'paenitentia', which I sought to pretend in the presence of God and try to express with a fictitious and forced love, now nothing sounds sweeter or more gracious to me than 'paenitentia'; for thus the precepts of God become sweet to us when we understand them, not only by reading books but in the wounds of the most sweet saviour.

There again you see the late medieval, spiritually committed pastor and the source of all that theology which was to become so ebullient; ebullient simply because he felt so strongly about it.

However many of Luther's finer theological points were lost on the majority of his followers. Bob Scribner says that as far as most people were concerned, they had been told that they no longer needed the saints, so they set about removing their statues. They were told that they did not need to pay for indulgences, and so they stopped paying. They were told that the clergy were probably the agents of the antichrist, so some of them went through the streets thinking 'Why not beat up a priest for Christ?'

Inevitably, matters got out of hand, and there were riots. All of this began to worry Luther. He was aware of the danger of teaching people habits which, once learnt, would not be easy to cast off afterwards. So, for example, when he came to the question of images, he said that images were idolatrous but that although there were probably too many of them, people must not be encouraged to go out and take action on their own for fear of engendering general lawlessness and rebellion.

At first, then, there was a great surge of enthusiasm for all sorts of new ideas in religion, but soon it started to outstrip Luther's particular set of parameters; Luther wanted to go so far, and no further. When people started profaning the host or mocking the Mass, Luther's reaction was to say that although the priest probably deserved some robust criticism, there were limits. But he was unable to stop people from hurling rocks through parsons' windows, or sometimes taking more extreme action. One man in Augsburg bared his behind at the host in the tabernacle, saying 'Fie on you, Christ, what are you doing in that little house?'

On the one hand, therefore, there was a certain amount of what might best be termed eccentric loutishness. On the other, you find some examples of behaviour which clearly show that people were also acting out the old forms of religion, but with a new twist. For instance, if you take an image of the Pope, throw it in the mud and then carry it through the streets, all you are doing is acting out a ritual purification transformed into a ritual of profanation.

So there were twin movements – deconstruction and construction. It must be remembered that the earlier reformers did not set out to create a new Church. They set out to show what was wrong with the old one, but while they were busy doing that, the old Church started to come apart at the seams. So when these reformers turned round and said that they did not want to celebrate the Mass in the old way, they found that people began doing away with vestments as well, and began to put the host into people's hands rather than on their tongues. The first time that was done, one communicant was so terrified that he dropped it and ran out of the church. The radicals said that they wanted to give the cup of communion wine to the laity, as part of the process of getting them used to handling things hitherto regarded as sacred objects. Many people were not happy with such drastic change, and Luther himself backed away from a new, radical communion service. In fact, he came up with something that looked very much like the old papal form of the Mass.

So for many within the reform tradition, the essentials of the religious life – the Mass, communion and the liturgy – looked very much as they did before the Reformation, and this was true right up to the middle of the sixteenth century. There were still large quantities of Latin to listen to or simply to sit through; there was still a priest wearing vestments, still candles on the altar. At the consecration the priest still spoke special words – admittedly in German, this time – elevated the little white wafer and had bells rung. To the congregation, it would all have looked exactly as it did under the papacy.

The underlying theology had, of course, changed but most of the populace was not terribly aware of the fact. In 1543 a Lutheran pastor described how, in his church, the people stood outside the church chattering all the time. When they heard the sacristy bell, they took a look inside and saw the host elevated, and believed that they had received the sacrament through viewing it. Then they went home. This parallels the popular misunderstanding of the Mass which was so prevalent before the Reformation. It was only in 1543 that the Lutheran theologians in Wittenberg, including Melancthon, professor of Greek and representative of Luther in his absence, started to question the elevation of the host, suggesting that it should be abolished since it led people to believe in transubstantiation, that is to believe that the priest turns the bread and wine on the table into the body and blood of Christ. They set about abolishing it, but met a great deal of popular resistance.

Luther could not contain what he had started. However, there were compensations too. He and Katie were ensconced in the old priory where he had been a monk. He had become an institution. Ian Siggins says that because Katie was such a good housekeeper, and a hard working, thrifty manager of the Luther farms and gardens – and a devoted mother to boot – that Luther came to rely on her a great deal. He enjoyed inviting squads of students and colleagues from the faculty at the university round to the cloister where they lived, night after night. They would sit and sing lute songs while the great man let pearls of wisdom fall from his lips.

Sometimes there would be banter between him and Katie in the presence of the students. One night, when he was talking to the students, Katie walked in and he said, 'The time will come when a man will take more than one wife' (tact was not, perhaps, Luther's stongest trait), and she shot back 'The devil believe that!' Luther persisted, saying that a wife could only bear one child a year, while a husband could beget many. She retorted, 'But Paul says every man should have his own wife', to which Luther replied, 'His own, yes, but not the only one – that's not in Paul'. They often had exchanges in a similar vein, and during this 'Table Talk' the students would jot down what they heard the old man say, whether worthy or not.

The 'Table Talk' is a somewhat confusing source because when people, especially students, write down that kind of overheard remark from an honoured teacher they do not always get it right and there is always the temptation to put a gloss on what one has heard. It is not, therefore, the most reliable of sources – but it does, nevertheless, give a very clear flavour of Luther's personality.

Luther had a strong character. He was an impetuous and idealistic man, but he was not a meticulous planner or a perfectionist. Neither was he always consistent. But he was honest about the shortcomings in the reforms he had inspired. It is worth remembering Patrick Collinson's remark that Luther observed that life was worse with the reformers than with the papists, but that it did not particularly worry him. He never expected the things of this world to be perfect or even merely satisfactory. He was attending to what he considered to be the heart of the matter.

Firstly, he was trying to make sense of the Bible, particularly the theology of St Paul and the material in the Book of Psalms. Secondly, he was an anxious Christian who had been brought up in a rather hot-house atmosphere, where it was contrition which was going to have to save him from death and hell. This concern becomes particularly significant if you remember that two of Luther's brothers died when he was very young. Death was always present, and how could he be sure that he was truly contrite? Thirdly, he was also a pastor running his parish in Wittenberg, preaching to his people hearing their confessions, and when Johann Tetzel arrived selling his pieces of parchment from Rome – for a consideration, of course – which would secure the remission of the penalties of sin, Luther was sure that this was a lie. It was grace on the cheap – or relatively cheap – and Luther knew that grace was expensive and hard and difficult to attain.

It may be that this crisis forced him towards the proposition that there is nothing that we can do to help ourselves in the slightest way to get on the right side of the ledger so far as God is concerned. On the contrary, all our efforts to improve ourselves and to please God are so self-serving that they are positively counter-productive. Luther saw the condition of man as *curvatus in se* – curved in upon himself. He believed that the essence of sin is self-esteem, self-preservation and self-love; therefore one can only be saved by something done entirely for God, something outside oneself. It is this which brings about a proper relationship with God and, by definition, it happens all at once, not by slow degrees and through effort.

That mood of self-criticism was not limited to the Luther. Rome held its own reforming council, the fifth Lateran Council. This passed many reforming decrees but the whole process seemed to lack impetus. According to Eamon Duffy the papacy which had survived the squabbles of the anti-popes and the antics of the Borgias was now prey to a more subtle menace.

The real disaster for the papacy was the fact that during the second half of the fifteenth century in particular, it ceased to be primarily a body claiming universal spiritual jurisdiction and became an Italian principality first and foremost instead. The turning point, perhaps, occurs towards the end of that century, when the business of the papal curia ceased to be transacted in Latin and began to be conducted in Italian.

So the popes could now be seen by devout Catholics – such as Thomas More – as essentially Italian princes who did have a spiritual claim on Catholics, but it was a claim which needed to be contained and narrowly defined because a far more important aspect of the papacy was its dynastic and warlike preoccupations. It is ironic that Thomas More advised Henry VIII against making too many enthusiastic pro-papal statements during the 1520s precisely because he thought it likely that, in the near future, the king might be at odds politically with the papacy. It is ironic, too, that Thomas More was eventually to die over the issue of whether the pope or the king was the head of the Church in England.

It is easy to tidy up the past. The truth is less manageable. In Luther's day, as in our own, people's beliefs were complex. Many Catholics believed in the need for reform, but many reformers would seem Catholic by today's standards. And there was a further complication. The reformers found themselves confronting deep-rooted ideas which were older than Christianity. Bob Scribner says that before the Reformation, many people had their own collections of spells and charms. If you had a sick horse, you would say a spell over it – usually a set of prayers invoking the saints combined with signs of the cross and, perhaps, include the use of healing herbs like juniper.

The reformers tried to get rid of these practices, condemning them as superstitious. Johann Agricola, the German reformer and former pupil of Luther, even wrote a set of new prayers which say 'Trust in God and your health will improve'. But people still used the old spells in the countryside. The reformed clergy even connived with them by allowing reformation spells and charms. These contained no references to the saints;

instead, they invoked the Trinity or Christ, but they were still essentially magic spells.

There are two landmarks in this battle against ancient belief. In 1636, the protestant pastor in a country parish became so fed up with the way in which his parishioners used these spells that he put the spells together in a collection. It was the first printed collection of such material, and the result was that they became more generally known. Secondly, there was the case towards the end of the seventeenth century of the Swabian pastor who for forty years worked in a couple of little parishes trying to eradicate these superstitions until, finally, he had a nervous breakdown and gave up. In a sense, this indicates how frustrated the clergy became over this issue.

One particular spell that annoyed the pastor intensely involved binding up the leg of a chair, with all kinds of magical injunctions, as a means of curing all sorts of maladies of the human leg. He heard of one parishioner who had done this, and he went to her and said, 'Look, it really is no good doing this; God does not work like that.' His parishioner simply replied that it had worked. This rather stumped him and all he could think to say, rather lamely, was that it must have been the work of the devil.

This idea of a magical universe goes right back to the early years of the Reformation, and it may well go back to Luther's stance on the Eucharist. Luther wanted to preserve transubstantiation. He wanted to keep some idea of the ability of the divine to intervene in the natural world and change it. That stance sold the pass so far as getting rid of magic was concerned, and so long as there was this kind of ambiguity in Lutheranism, then much of the old, magical and sacramental world view could continue to hold sway.

Many reformers would be more radical than Luther, although often using his ideas as their initial inspiration. Others arrived independently at very similar conclusions. Among these was a quick-witted Swiss priest called Ulrich Zwingli, the forgotten man of the Reformation, who had been a military chaplain and was the recipient of a papal pension. He ended up as the first great Swiss reformer and advocate of the idea of a national church. Ironically it was the papal pension which led him to reform. He used the money to buy books by Erasmus. Alistair Duke, Senior Lecturer in History at the University of Southampton, says those books proved to be the major turning point in Zwingli's life.

His great moment came when, in 1516, he acquired Erasmus' translation of the New Testament. By this time, it seems that he had become fairly fluent in Greek anyway, but the scales fell from his eyes once he was able to read this new translation. Throughout his life he was a tremendous admirer of Erasmus. It is clear that he regarded 1516 as the decisive year in his life, and that is – at least in part – why he always wanted to maintain his independence from Luther. He said that he had not really heard anything of Luther before 1518, and so he felt that it was rather unfair that he was being tarred with the Lutheran brush when he had his own, independent insights. He began to preach on the authority of scripture and on the distinction between the spirit and the flesh, a distinction that he probably acquired partly from his knowledge of late medieval theology. It must be remembered that in the decade between 1515 and 1525 – after the time of the Peasants' War in Germany – there was tremendous intellectual ferment. Zwingli himself spoke about it being a golden age. Others talked about Christ living again.

Luther fits into this pattern, and he emerges as one of the leading figures of this period.

There are some people who are *not* there. Before the reformation there seemed to be a steady stream of remarkable visionary women – Catherine of Siena, Hildegard of Bingen, Bridget of Sweden – ready to advise and to admonish priests and popes. Where are the reforming women? Elsie McKee, Professor of History at Princeton, New Jersey believes they existed but have been ignored. She cites one example – Katerina, the wife of the former priest turned reformer Matthew Zell.

Katerina came from the city of Strasbourg, and grew up as a Catholic. Elsie McKee says that Katerina's early childhood, according to her own description, sounds very much the same as Martin Luther's. She was constantly unhappy about not being sure of her salvation, although she did a great many good works and went to church often. When she read about what Luther was teaching, she said that she felt as if she had been drawn from hell to heaven. The sense of freedom from having to pay for her sins also gave her a sense of gratitude, which expressed itself in her engaging in more work than ever. One of the first things that she did as a protestant was to marry a priest which was in itself quite a courageous act. Any woman who married a priest was letting herself in for gossip and slander. However, Katerina was very much more articulate than most other women of her time, and wrote in defence of clerical marriage. That

IESVS · MAT · XI ·

VENITE AD ME · QVI   LABORATIS · &EGO REFICIĀ VOS ·

HVLDRICVS · ZVINGLIVS ·

ANNO ÆTATIS · 44 ·

· B ·

*Ulrich Zwingli, the papal pensioner and the forgotten man of the
Reformation who was theologically more radical than Luther*

was not something that a woman and layperson was supposed to do, but that did not stop her.

Also, in the first year of her marriage, she and her husband Matthew set up their household and straight away began to take in all sorts of refugees, people who were uprooted because of the religious troubles of the time. Nor did she stop there. In the same week that she took in the first group of refugees, she also wrote a pastoral letter to the wives they had left behind, and it was published.

She also saw that mothers were unable to teach their children simply because they themselves had not been well taught. Her husband wrote a catechism for the children and Katerina published a hymn book with some good songs for them. She felt that the songs they had been singing to their children were improper and unedifying and thought it important that ordinary people should be able to sing the gospel to their children. Her concern for children was poignant – none of her own had survived infancy.

Katerina was probably more outspoken than many of her contemporaries, but the fact that she and her husband formed a pastoral team was not so unusual. She was much more his colleague than simply his wife or housekeeper. She certainly considered herself a colleague of the other reformers, and was very proud of the fact that her husband did not particularly worry if the house was not properly looked after when she was out visiting in the parish.

Some people found Katerina rather outrageous because she took in people they considered heretics, fed them and defended them. She was ready to give shelter and food even to those she disagreed with. She was fond of quoting the story of Balaam the soothsayer and his ass, from the Book of Numbers, which describes how the ass sees an angel standing in his path, but Balaam does not. The ass moves out of the way so that the angel will not kill Balaam, who cannot see it and thinks the ass is simply being disobedient. When he urges the ass forward for the third time, it says, 'Look, there is the angel', at which point Balaam suddenly sees it and realises that the ass is the one who has been inspired by God, not him. Sometimes Katerina would refer to herself as Balaam's ass, and would say that it was not always the learned men who understood scripture best; she was sure that she was the one who saw the angel, not them.

The Reformation was the work of many hands. Luther was its catalyst but not its culmination. Some of the changes immediately associated with the reformation within the liturgy are more the responsibility of Zwingli, the forgotten man. Alistair Duke points out that under Luther, the Latin Mass was translated but the order of service remained relatively unchanged. Zwingli, on the other hand, introduced a communion service where all the participants sat at tables. It was a meal of thanksgiving and a major corporate event. In an extraordinary way Zwingli, although he repudiated the Catholic teaching of transubstantiation, taught that an act of transubstantiation nevertheless took place within the congregation. During the time they were participating in the communion service, *they* were transformed into the body of Christ. This idea survives as his contribution to reform protestantism.

But for many, Luther was revolutionary enough, among them Thomas More, the Christian humanist and friend of Erasmus. Anthony Kenny, warden of Rhodes House, Oxford, explains that More thought that Luther was someone who had been unfaithful to his own vows, and had encouraged other people to be unfaithful to theirs; that he did not believe many doctrines which were an essential part of the Christian message, and that he was disrupting the unity of Christendom as well as disrupting the proper relationship between Church and State. More and Luther wrote books against each other, and they do not make happy reading. They were extremely rude to each other, and the books are full of rather low grade, childish abuse. In fact, it would be easier to admire Luther and More if they had never written anything about each other.

Occasionally Luther's pen outstripped charity and prudence, but without it and the printing press the history of the Christian family would have been very different. His massive achievements overshadow any personal shortcomings. Patrick Collinson maintains that Luther was a religious genius who penetrated to the inner truth of Biblical Christianity as no other Christian teacher has, although someone like Zwingli had great capacity in terms of organising a coherent, civic reformation.

In speaking of Luther the man, however, it must be admitted that he was far from perfect. There are quite a few things which are hard to accept, such as his anti-semitism and the vulgarity of his attacks on the papists. But in a sense, that is the point. He was not a man of religion in the conventional, hagiographical fashion. What he insisted on, above all, is that God is involved in material concerns, and that is where He is to be found – nowhere else. Luther actually wrote the carol 'Away in a Manger' saying, in effect: I will not have God except as that baby in that manger.

In a sense, too, Luther said: I will not have God except in the flesh and blood which is communicated to me in the bread and wine of the Mass. He took the Real Presence very seriously. He strongly believed that God is mixed up in all our human affairs and hides himself in them so that, although the world is full of terrible and unacceptable things, God is to be found there too.

Luther would not have claimed to be a saint; it is his humanity which makes him outstanding. As a religious leader he belongs right at the top. He lived for the Christian ideal and for the beauty of the Gospels. His last recorded words were no self-confident battle cry but a profound statement of the faith of a humble and simple believer. He said, 'We are all beggars – that is the truth.'

CHAPTER III

A KING, A WITCH AND SOME MARTYRS

'Monks, monks, monks, monks.'

Henry VIII

The final defiant words, according to some, of Henry VIII – the king famed for his wives and for his flamboyance, a man who outfaced the Pope and, by founding the Church of England, gave his people a sense of independence and nationhood which would last for centuries and sustain an empire. *Or* – to put it another way – the last cry of a religious conservative and a superstitious hypochondriac who throughout his life was tormented by biblical scruples and racked by sexual guilt.

Whichever you prefer, the fact remains that for England, the catalyst for religious reform was not Ockham with his razor or Tyndale with his Bible but Henry Tudor, Defender of the Faith and King of England, Wales and Ireland; a cruel, romantic and insecure character who as a young man was a pious and traditional Catholic until, it was rumoured, he fell under the spell of a six-fingered witch.

The story of reform in England is unlike any of its continental counterparts. It is a saga of heroism and hatred, muddle and martyrdom, high in court drama rather than intellectual ferment. While experiments with radical theology were being pursued by popular demand in the towns and cities of Europe, in England reform was imposed from above. When Henry acceded to the throne of England in 1509 he did not, contrary to popular belief, find himself ruling a country seething with religious indignation. Dr Eamon Duffy explains that for most people the Church was their parish church, and in most parts of western Europe, and certainly in England, the laity were in charge of the parish church. They controlled the financial affairs of the parish. In England the guilds were of immense importance. These were religious and trade associations for lay people which raised money, organised ritual celebrations and had several annual beanfeasts. This was all an essential part of parish social life. Guilds also organised elaborate processions, put on religious plays and, very often, employed clergy to say Masses for them. This meant many lay people were by and large in control of their own religious lives. There was real enthusiasm and commitment behind religious practice. For example, in England many townspeople would regularly go to Mass not just on Sundays but once or twice during the week.

If a parish was controlled by a great monastery the situation was likely to be less happy. The abbot would have a degree of control over what went on in his parishes, and in these cases lay people would find themselves excluded from control of parish life. This was, not unnaturally, a recipe for discontent. The average man in the village alehouse in 1500 *might* hear rumours of scandalous goings-on at Rome, but Rome was a long way away. The local squire might occasionally have contact with Rome or he would be able to afford to go on pilgrimage to Rome, or he might want to marry a first cousin and would need a dispensation from Rome to do it. But on the whole the Pope did not impinge much on the lives of ordinary people, so it is not likely that the ills or otherwise of the papacy would have been much of a topic for conversation in pubs – not until the Pope and the King began to fight. Then it was a different matter.

The reasons for that fight were, to begin with, unashamedly dynastic. Henry had not expected to sit on the throne of England. The death of Prince Arthur, his elder brother, changed all that. At eighteen Henry inherited not only the throne but also the 24-year-old Catherine of Aragon, Arthur's widow. This enforced marriage was a disaster. They had five children out of whom three boys and one girl failed to survive infancy. Only one girl, Mary, showed any sign of thriving. This began to prey on Henry's mind. Dr Susan Brigden, fellow of Lincoln College, Oxford, says Henry, although given by temperament to self-delusion, was sincere in his belief that the failure to have a male heir was a sign of divine displeasure on him and upon that marriage. He was probably already thinking of ways to have the Aragon marriage annulled even before he met Anne Boleyn. And Henry, being Henry, with his interest

Henry Tudor, Defender of the Faith, a religious traditionalist who was romantic, cruel, insecure and paranoid

in theology, found a text in Leviticus which suggested that the man who marries his brother's wife will be childless because it was a forbidden relationship. As soon as he met Anne he began to think about annulment with an obsessive determination. From 1527 until their marriage early in 1533 Anne and Henry thought of themselves as betrothed and began planning ways of being married, and those ways in the end involved no less than the sundering of Catholic Christendom, the breaking of Rome and the denial of papal authority within England.

It was said that Henry was literally bewitched by Anne. She had six fingers on one hand, supposedly a sign of witchcraft, and many people blamed her for all the changes in the 1530s. Certainly Henry was in her power. As shown in his letters to her, he was infatuated by her, and by 1527 she became a kind of insistent theme in everything he thought and did.

It was clear that Anne would not be his mistress. She had a sister who had already been the King's mistress, and Anne learnt from her sister's 'kindness'. She was determined to be queen. There was a marvellous moment when a play was performed at court in 1528, with Anne playing Perseverance and her sister Mary, the ex-mistress, playing Kindness – 'kindness' almost as another word for easy virtue. Anne was determined not to be merely the King's mistress.

By any standards Anne Boleyn, or Bullen, as she is sometimes called, was exceptional. She was the niece of the Duke of Norfolk, but she had an edge on the other eligible ladies of the court. She had spent some time in Flanders as lady-in-waiting to Margaret of Austria. She had also been at the French court. She had style, but as well as continental panache she had picked up reformist ideas. She was to have an unlikely ally in the cautious, near-sighted Thomas Cranmer, an apparently undistinguished man, who in the end would die a hero. After a run of the mill career at Cambridge, Cranmer was suddenly made Archbishop of Canterbury. Why did Henry choose him? Was he aware he was picking a reformist dark horse? Dr Diarmaid MacCulloch of Wesley College, Bristol says that what Henry liked about Cranmer was that he was prepared to be a tool in the divorce plans. Cranmer had provided arguments and did much of the paperwork; that was Cranmer's only virtue as far as Henry was concerned. He was completely unaware that Cranmer was a Lutheran sympathiser. Anne Boleyn was also in favour of reform and knew about Cranmer's views because she was the centre of a circle which rapidly emerged as reformist. But from Henry's point of view, soundness on the divorce front was much more important than fashionable theology.

Like Anne, Cranmer had continental links. His second wife, Margaret, was the niece of a prominent German Lutheran theologian. Cranmer-the-cautious married her when he was a fully ordained priest, risking both ecclesiastical and royal anger. This bold move was a sign of reforms to come. Meanwhile Cranmer worked away steadily on Henry's behalf but to little avail. Rome would not allow Henry to set aside Catherine of Aragon so Henry set aside Rome. He declared himself Head of the Church of England, closed the monasteries and seized their assets. But plausible expediency and greed have little to do with reform. Henry remained by temperament a traditional Catholic. But he was being educated. Susan Brigdon explains that it was Anne who showed him, for instance, William Tyndale's *The Obedience of a Christian Man*. William Tyndale was an exile, a heretic, and for Henry to be reading his works was extraordinary. She had also shown him other virulently anticlerical books which she had received from her friends in evangelical circles in London.

The image of Henry as a gentle troubadour king with a penchant for reform is false. Anne would eventually fall prey to his dark paranoia and religious superstitions. By the time she and Henry married, she was pregnant. The child was a girl, Elizabeth. Anne became pregnant again. This time she miscarried and the stillborn child was deformed. Anne's fate was sealed. Yet again Henry saw divine disfavour behind the tragedy. He persuaded Cranmer to preside over a court annulling the Boleyn marriage. This was done and Anne was executed. It may seem strange that Cranmer did not stand up for the Queen with whom, in theological terms, he had been so much in sympathy and his acquiescence in the Boleyn execution did much to give him the reputation of being a time-serving survivor.

Diarmaid MacCulloch says that although Cranmer went along with the execution of Anne and also that of Thomas Cromwell on trumped-up charges, it must also be said that in each case he wrote a personal letter to Henry pleading him 'Show mercy. If the charges against these people are true, then punish them. But if they are not true, show mercy, and in all cases remember that you are a sinner'. These were extraordinarily brave letters to write to a man like Henry, and a sign of the courage which in the end led Cranmer to a martyr's death.

Sixteenth-century England would see many martyrs, not all of them well remembered today. Henry would marry four more times. His final wife Catherine Parr was as convinced a reformer as Anne Boleyn. As he grew older Henry's religious conservatism came more to the fore. Catherine Parr herself almost came to the executioner's block when it was found she had connections with Anne Askew, a dangerous reformer who had great influence in court circles, particularly among the court women. Anne had fled from Lincolnshire to London to escape an unhappy marriage.

Susan Brigdon says that Anne Askew came to be a controversial figure within the reformist network because she not only read the Bible but speculated on it as well. She also held more radical ideas on the Mass – she insisted that it was only a commemoration of Christ's death and nothing more. She was dangerous because she was connected to people in high places at court – her brothers were part of the King's Privy Chamber. She had friends in low places too, among the London apprentices, and she also seems to have been connected with some very radical groups indeed.

In today's language Anne was a protestant – an anachronistic label. Henry was certainly far from being a reformer but what about Cranmer with all his Lutheran sympathies? Diarmaid MacCulloch advises against hasty labelling. He points out that the word 'Protestantism' had only been invented three years before Cranmer was made Archbishop so it is difficult to pinpoint Cranmer's beliefs. The best way of analysing the matter is to identify two broad schools of thought about the Church of the early 1530s. It is a question of reform or defence: on one side there are people who feel that it is more important to reform the Church than it is to defend it; on the other side, there is the group who feel that it is much more important to defend the Church than to reform it. All we can say about Cranmer is that he falls into the first of these categories. He felt that reforming the Church was more important than defending it. Beyond that, since he had married the niece of a Lutheran theologian, he had many Lutheran friends, but over the course of time his views diverged significantly from those of Luther.

The great litmus test in theology in the sixteenth century was how you viewed the Communion service. At one end of the scale you have the traditional view of transubstantiation, maintaining that the words of the Last Supper were literally true and therefore the priest turns the bread and wine on the table into the body and blood of Christ. At the other end of the scale, you have people who saw the communion service merely as a memorial – an act which recalls Christ's having sacrificed his life on the cross for all humanity. There is a vast scale of difference between these two views of what a Eucharist is. We can see through little fragments of evidence from Cranmer's life how he moved from the first position, creating God from bread and wine, through to the memorial position. It took him years. In the 1530s he was still very much with the old theology, which was Luther's theology just as much as the Pope's, yet during the 1540s we can be quite certain that Cranmer moved beyond this position. He lost his belief in what's been called 'the Real Presence' in the Eucharistic elements, and takes it through what he called later 'the spiritual presence', that is a true presence depending on belief, not transubstantiation. That is taking it far beyond the world of even Luther, far beyond the world of the Pope, far more towards the world of Swiss theologians like Zwingli.

Cranmer welcomed Henry's break with Rome because he was convinced the Pope was an obstacle to reform. Others were not so sure – most notable among them Thomas More who had succeeded Cardinal Wolsey to the Lord Chancellorship. More felt he could not swear the various oaths of allegiance demanded by Henry. He would end up dying for his principles. Dr Anthony Kenny, Warden of Rhodes House, Oxford, says More was motivated most of all by his horror at seeing the united Christendom fractured. More saw the whole European community of Catholics as being a single entity which was more important than the national identity of one particular country. He was very much a European, although also a very proud Englishman. He thought that what one should be proud of was England's place as part of the general Christian Commonwealth. It was the time when local nationalisms were rising all over Europe and More was against that. It is true that he eventually died for the Pope, but he did not believe in the papacy in the same way as, say, a Catholic would have done in the 1920s and 1930s when Thomas More was eventually canonised by the Catholic Church as a martyr. After the First Vatican Council in 1869, the papacy was put very much on a pedestal as the head of the Church in its own right, and no matter what the other bishops might feel, the pope could lay down the law. That was not More's view. He was living at a time when the popes were a pretty sorry, shabby and occasionally wicked lot, but he believed that they were the vicars of Christ, and therefore, however bad vicars they might be, you had to put up with them. And even though he died for the Pope, it was once said that if you told More that he was going to be a martyr for a Christian doctrine, and then you told him it was going to be for the authority of the Pope, he would have groaned. It would have been the least of all Christian doctrines that he would have wanted to die for. He would have loved to die for the sacraments or the Real Presence on the altar or the unity of Christendom.

Thomas More was beheaded for treason in 1535. In terms of religious belief he and Anne Askew had little in common but they were to share a similar fate. Anne would be burnt for heresy. Susan Brigdon explains that towards the end of Henry VIII's reign the theological conservatives in high places determined to use Anne Askew as an instrument to bring down their opponents at the court. In the Tower in 1546 she was tortured on the rack, which was not part of correct English legal procedure. When the news came out it shocked people. But not only was Anne racked, she was racked by the Lord Chancellor and by Sir Richard Riche, the man who had betrayed Sir Thomas More, and the questions they asked her were very revealing – 'Who sent you money in the Tower? Was it the Countess of Hertford? Was it my Lady Denny?' – these were desperate days in politics. Henry VIII was not long for this world, and everyone knew that when he died he would leave a son who was a minor, and that the faction which was in power at Henry VIII's death could not only control the realm for their purposes, as a regency over the young Prince, Edward VI to be, but they could also determine the religion in a new reign. They could determine whether England went further in the protestant direction of reform or reverted to Catholicism. This was a time of hard actions and harsh words. The Ballad of Anne Askew pulled no punches.

> I saw a royal throne
> Where Justice should have sitt
> But in her stead was one
> Of modye, cruel wit
>
> Absorbed was righteousness
> As of the raging flood
> Satan in his excess
> Sucked up the guiltless blood

No prizes for guessing who was the monarch 'of cruel wit'.

Away from the court, matters were less intense. In theory the Reformation proper was established in England in 1533 by Act of Parliament. But official dates can be misleading. As far as the man in the sixteenth century pew was concerned, Eamon Duffy says the Reformation began when people noticed it. In the early 1530s Henry VIII broke with the Papacy, but there is a set of church wardens' accounts for Stanford-in-the-Vale, a little parish in Berkshire, which tell a different story. From the 1550s the church wardens there kept a record of the repairs done to the damage caused by the Reformation. They were writing during Queen Mary's reign, when Catholicism was being restored. They date what they call the 'wicked time of schism' from the second year of King Edward VI that is, seventeen or eighteen years after the break with Rome. They dated it from then because that was the year when the Mass was abolished and they began to have the English Communion services. It is as if that was the year when the people of Stanford-in-the-Vale first noticed the Reformation had happened. So for them, as for many like them, it was an event which took place long after the official break with Rome.

The people of Stanford-in-the-Vale had a point. Reform did not really take root until the death of Henry and the accession of the frail boy-king Edward. Cranmer, assisted by Ridley and Latimer, framed England's new faith. After six short manipulated years on the throne, Edward was clearly not for this world. To protect the reforms he had nurtured, cautious Cranmer took a gamble which would cost him his life. Diarmaid MacCulloch explains that Edward and his advisers were horrified at the thought of a Catholic successor, Mary, coming to the throne, so they diverted the succession to Lady Jane Grey, and Cranmer was part of that scheme. He was somewhat unhappy about it, but went along with it. He signed all the relevant documents, and when the attempt to divert the succession failed he was labelled a traitor. Another reason for this was that Queen Mary decided that he was the chief symbol of everything that had gone wrong in England over the previous twenty years.

It must be said that he could have fled in the opening months of Mary's reign, but he did not. He stayed around, and was arrested and imprisoned. From the last months of 1553 to his death in March 1556 he was a prisoner in the hands of Mary's government. He was put on trial and declared a traitor and heretic. With all that crushing weight of condemnation on his shoulders, he faced martyrdom. In his last months it

*Cranmer the cautious becomes Cranmer the reforming hero as he
steadfastly endures a martyr's death, the victim
of Mary Tudor's thirst for revenge*

is quite clear that he was a desperately lonely man, a man whose friends were dying at the stake, and in the end his nerve cracked. Cranmer made the greatest mistake any prisoner can make: he made friends with his jailor.

In his loneliness he listened to the Catholic jailor telling him that he must recant to save his soul. In that state of moral confusion, and perhaps guilt over his betrayal of Mary, he signed a whole series of recantations, which he believed would save him from the stake. But what made Cranmer in the end a martyr was Mary's sheer determination to punish him as the man who humiliated her mother. She would not allow him to escape the stake, and in the end Cranmer realized he would die. When he came to the University Church in Oxford he had most probably already made up his mind to reject the recantations he had signed. He had a set text in front of him. In effect, he had to preach a sermon at his own funeral. But he departed from that text. He said all the good pious things at the beginning, asking people to pray for him as a sinner and so on and so forth, but at the end he condemned the Mass and shouted in the middle of the church, 'I believe as I said in my book against the Bishop of Winchester' – and that book had been a condemnation of the Mass. There was uproar in the church. He was silenced, dragged out to the stake, and at the stake once more continued his symbolic rejection of his own recantation. In effect, he saved his integrity in a way that he had never done before, with an extraordinary courage – courage perhaps born of desperation. A vivid account is given by John Foxe in his *Book of Martyrs*. Foxe, of course, was a Protestant witness, but we know from other Catholic accounts that this is very much like the truth. This is how Foxe put it:

'And when the wood was kindled, and the fire began to burn near him, he put his right hand into the flame which he held so steadfast and immovable, saving that once with the same hand he wiped his face, that all men might see his hand burned before his body was touched. His body did so abide the burning of the flame with such constancy and steadfastness that standing always in the one place without moving his body he seemed to move no more than the stake to which he was bound. His eyes were lifted up into heaven and oftentimes he repeated "His unworthy right hand", so long as his voice would suffer him. And using often the words of Stephen, "Lord Jesus, receive my spirit", in the greatness of the flame, he gave up the ghost.'

Cranmer had certainly been influenced by Luther but he, Ridley and Latimer had also absorbed ideas from Calvin, the formidable organiser of Geneva. In a roundabout way Henry's conservatism had forged links between England and continental Calvinists. Men, like John Hooper, the English reformer, who had fled Henry's England, were sheltered by Calvinists and then returned during Edward's reign. It was Calvin rather than Luther who set the tone of much of English religious life, once Mary's attempt to bludgeon her country back to Catholicism failed.

Calvin of Geneva was a rather forbidding figure who comes over as a much colder man than Luther. Possibly, according to Elsie McKee, this was because he was a thwarted French academic who did not want to lead or even stay in Geneva. She says he felt he had been tricked by God during what was intended to be a brief stopover.

Geneva had been in something of an uproar. They had thrown out their Catholic bishops and were being reformed by a fiery red-headed man named Guillaume Farel, but Farel was more of an exciting preacher than an organiser, so Geneva was rather chaotic. He had read Calvin's *Institutes of the Christian Religion*, and was impressed. He decided Calvin was the man he needed to help him organise the Geneva reformation.

He asked Calvin to stay and help. Calvin said he did not want to, but Farel threatened to call down God's curses on Calvin's peace and quiet if he left Geneva in its hour of need. Calvin wanted to leave Geneva. He did not want to live a public life, but he believed that Farel was telling him what God needed him to do for the sake of other people, and that was more important than his personal preferences. So Calvin stayed in Geneva until he and Farel were exiled several years later. Before Calvin could breathe a sigh of relief Martin Luther decided to call Calvin to Strasbourg to look after the French refugees. Strasbourg was a German-speaking city but close enough to France to have many French-language Protestants. Martin Luther had to do what Farel did – he insisted that he would call down God's curses on Calvin's peace and quiet if Calvin didn't comply, so Calvin went to Strasbourg for several years.

It turned out to be a very enjoyable three years, but after he had been there for only two years the Genevans decided to call Calvin back as they had not been able to find a good pastor. Calvin demurred quite firmly, but the reformers in other Protestant cities thought that Geneva could not continue to organise the Church without Calvin. There really was not a strong pastor to help them. They were afraid the Church would collapse if they did not have Calvin back, so again there was much arm-twisting, but this time it took about a year. Calvin finally went back to Geneva, and spent the rest of his minstry there; but given that kind of story it is possible to see why perhaps Calvin's temper was not of the best.

In the event Calvin drafted the constitution of the new Genevan republic. This, together with his *Institutes of Religion*, would give him a reputation across Europe as a teacher with a practical vision of faith and civic life. Calvinism was famed for its discipline and organisation. It was not the only form of continental reform. While Calvin was putting the finishing touches to the reform, a more radical vision of Christianity was being mooted. The movement which held strongly to belief in adult not infant baptism spread widely through the German speaking part of Europe. Those in it were known by a variety of insulting epithets. The one which stuck was 'Anabaptists'. The Mennonite historian, Dr Alan Kreider explains that 'Anabaptist' means 're-baptizer'. Luther called them sneaks, corner-preachers and fanatics. They called themselves brothers and sisters, occasionally baptists, and as time went on they called themselves anabaptists.

When thinking about the Anabaptists, says Alan Kreider, you have to bear in mind that for virtually 1,200 years there had been a world in which to be European was, automatically, to be Christian; it was the same thing. And this meant that it was a society in which everyone was baptized shortly after birth, and everybody thought of himself as a Christian, except for those hardy nonconformists, the Jews, who maintained a kind of subsidiary presence throughout the history of Christendom, and as a result were frequently persecuted. Then in the 1520s a group of people began to question whether this was an authentic expression of the original vision of Christianity. They began to say that another kind of expression and experience of Christianity might be possible. In this new Christianity, people would belong to the Church not because of birth or compulsion but rather because of conscious, deliberate choice. The Anabaptists were a group of people who decided to separate faith from coercion and force, and to move out, as a result, from Christendom into the world of nonconformity. They were the first modern nonconformists.

The Anabaptists had few friends. They were persecuted by Catholics, who burnt them, and by reformed Christians, who preferred to drown or behead them. Virtually all the early Anabaptist leaders lost their lives. It is thought that no fewer than 4,300 Anabaptists were killed for their faith. One of the main principles of the movement was pacifism. Michael Smith explains that they believed that the sword was an ordinance of God outside the perfection of Christ: the princes and rulers of this world are ordained for the punishment of evil-doers and for putting them to death, but within the perfection of Christ excommunication is the ultimate punishment and death is excluded. Because of that view they also held that going to war over matters of faith was not something that a Christian should be involved in. They stood by this very firmly, feeling – quite rightly, that far from being called upon to beat people up, the Christian was, if anything, called to be the one who suffered, as Christ had done. In fact, one of the great complaints they had against the established churches was, 'Where is the Cross? Where is the suffering that should be involved in being a follower of Christ?'.

The Anabaptists' belief in pacifism and redistribution of wealth was unlikely to recommend itself to secular rulers. On the other hand, Calvin has been accused of leaning too much towards an acceptance of capitalism. A justified criticism? Dr Alistair McGrath of Wycliff Hall, Oxford, explains that when Calvin arrived in Geneva the city was going through a period of liberation, and in order to survive it had to ensure that its economy was safe. Political survival depended on economic independence, and Geneva began a very capitalistic programme to try to establish its economy. Basically, Calvin laid a religious foundation which allowed you to become a capitalist and stay a good Christian at the same time. In Luther we have a rural reformer, someone operating in the backyard of Germany, reforming a very backward part of the country. The sort of major economic questions Calvin wrestled with would have been unknown to him, and Luther's economic thought, as far as the city was concerned, was very simple indeed; many scholars suggest that here was a typical medieval person, without any real sense of the economic forces that would shape modern Europe, whereas Calvin was living in a city which was going to be right in the forefront of the new economic revolution in Europe; he was aware of the way the wind was blowing and quite happy to go along with it.

There is always a battle between idealism and pragmatism for religious believers. In 1534 the Anabaptists of Munster in Westphalia forgot their

John Calvin, the reluctant reformer, badgered into organising unruly Geneva

pacifist principles when they found themselves surrounded by both Lutheran and Catholic armies. The people of Munster were defeated, tortured and killed. Alan Kreider believes that even in death they have been persecuted. Munster, he says, provides an illustration of the way in which the official Reformers have chosen to characterise the essence of the Anabaptist movement – as a movement that is essentially violent and psychologically disturbed. Munster was in fact an aberration as far as the Anabaptist movement was concerned. It was a movement in an episcopal city between 1533 and 1535 in which a group of people fired by an apocalyptic vision believed that the Kingdom of Heaven was going to descend very shortly, and descend through them.

On this basis they began to institute Old Testament cultural norms. They began to practise polygamy (partly because they needed to increase the population, because they were under pressure and under siege). They began to take to the sword, to defend themselves, and they represented the culmination of a movement of apocalyptic expectations. They were smashed by the forces of the Bishop of Munster, reinforced by others in a coalition against them, being defeated with great loss in 1535. For a few years other people kept up this violent vision and you find pockets of them here and there – barricading themselves in a cloister and bombarding their attackers with cheeses, or defending themselves with indiscriminate fire until they ran out of ammunition. But all this was not at all characteristic of the early period of the Anabaptist movement, nor was it characteristic of the movement after 1540 – it was an aberration which appeared comparatively suddenly. But it was a highly significant aberration, because it allowed the representatives of the dominant strands in Christian historiography to characterise the whole movement in terms of it, and thus enabled them to persecute even the memory of the Anabaptists.

Religious propaganda is not a new or rare phenomenon. Down the centuries, Calvin has had fairly negative publicity with the word 'Calvinist' often being used as shorthand for narrow-minded, unyielding faith. Does Calvin deserve better? Elsie McKee takes the view that Calvin has received a bad press and a reputation for grim thoroughness. Calvin was a second-generation reformer, and by that point there was a certain amount of confusion in the Protestant Reformation, so that the clarity and coherence which he brought to the movement were extremely important. He was not the pioneer and innovator that Luther was, but he had other gifts and one of them was being an incredibly clear, coherent, comprehensive teacher in a way that Luther was not.

Calvinism, through Cranmer, Ridley and Latimer, would leave its mark on England but all that lies in the future. After Henry the Catholic king who broke with Rome, after Edward the short-lived Protestant and Mary the much-hated Catholic, the country was punch drunk with religious feuding.

So what of Elizabeth Tudor and the English people? Anthony Kenny believes that there was then the middle-of-the-road Reformation of Queen Elizabeth, which was not as protestant as the Protestants would have liked, but equally not as papal as the Catholics would have liked. It collided with the newly reformed Roman Church, and a number of popes, particularly Pope Pius V and Pope Gregory XIII, attacked Queen Elizabeth by both religious and military means. Pius V excommunicated Elizabeth in 1570 in a famous papal bull entitled *Regnans in Excelsis* which released Roman Catholic subjects from their allegiance to her. He and his successors built up seminaries abroad – Pope Gregory XIII founded one at Douai and one in Rome – and these sent seminarists who had been ordained priests back to England as missionaries. Most of these were people who had nothing to do with military action or plots against the Queen. Many of them were executed for no other reason than that they were priests – it was made a capital offence to return to England if you had been ordained as a priest overseas.

Simultaneously with all this, there were a number of plots against Queen Elizabeth's life which had a certain degree of papal sanction. There were attempts to invade Ireland, and eventually, of course, the Spanish Armada, the most famous of all attempts to invade England. Philip II of Spain was the great supporter of the Pope's military ventures (though often a reluctant one), and the Spanish Armada was supposed to put a Catholic monarch on the throne. That failed, and then of course finally, after the reign of Elizabeth was over, there was the Gunpowder Plot. This was perceived as a Catholic plot though in fact it was not countenanced by anybody in Rome, nor even by the Jesuits (who by this time were the most effective missionaries in England), but none the less they got caught up in it.

The Gunpowder Plot marked the complete end of the Counter-Reformation's chances in England. The generation who had lived from, say, 1540 to 1610 would have seen at the beginning of their lives a

Catholic Queen burning Protestant bishops, then at the end of their lives they saw Catholic plotters trying to kill King, Lords and Commons, and then the feeling of the English people, which at the beginning of the sixteenth century had been one of the most Catholic in Europe, was that from then on England was a Protestant country. The Pope was the great enemy, the Jesuits were regarded as perfidious. The missionary priests, however personally innocent, were regarded as a Fifth Column sent by the Pope to corrupt the loyalty and patriotism of the English people. Rome had lost England.

CHAPTER IV

SOLDIERS, SAINTS AND SECOND THOUGHTS

'Moreover this is consulted of and concluded amongst the Jesuits, to send forth certain very audacious murderers who by poison may kill the principal doctors and teachers of the Evangelical and Calvinian Churches, and furnished with such great skill to poison, that they shall be able to infect dishes, saltcellars, basins, cauldrons and other vessels whatsoever appointed to daily use, that though they be twenty times wiped over and made clean, yet they shall retain the force of most deadly and present poison.'

Timely advice against inviting Jesuits to dinner published in 1609.

Long before there were reds under governmental beds, the Jesuits, a band of men pledged to follow Christ on the path of the Gospel, were the political and religious bogeymen of Protestant Europe. The early chapters in this book have looked at the Reformation through the eyes of those protesting against papal authority but there is another side to the story. Reform was afoot within the Catholic Church – reform *and* reaction to shattering events which had transformed the Christian Church in large parts of Western Europe.

Then, as now, it is a tempting nonsense to analyse the Catholic Church as a ruthlessly efficient single-minded papal machine. The story of reform in the Catholic Church is a story of bureaucratic skulduggery and of private idealism, of siege mentality and of courage, of narrow-mindedness and of prophetic insight. Above all it is a story of great individuals like Ignatius Loyola, the mystic ex-soldier who had wanted to live out his days in the Holy Land, Teresa of Avila, the dimpled nun inclined to laughter and levitation who re-organised her order and inspired the whole Church by her writings, and Matteo Ricci, sun dial designer and clock maker extraordinaire who took Christianity into the fabled forbidden city of the emperor of China. All these people and their disparate activities tend to be lumped under the title 'counter-reformation', an authoritative sounding eighteenth-century label but given the diversity of the sixteenth-century Catholic Church, does it really have any useful meaning?

According to Dr Anthony Kenny it meant two different things. First, it meant a kind of delayed and reactive reformation of the Roman Catholic Church itself. The rebellion of people like Luther against the authority of the Church was partly on doctrinal grounds, but it was very largely triggered off by the enormous corruption of the clergy in many parts of Europe, all the way from the papacy downwards. There had been several attempts to reform the Church – to make bishops live in their dioceses instead of comfortable courts, to make the parish clergy work harder at looking after their people, and to make monks and nuns keep their vows. Most of these attempts at reform ran into the sand in the fifteenth century. It was only when Christendom was brought up with a shock by the Reformation, with whole sections of Christendom separating themselves from the authority of the pope, that a real reformation got under way.

Many aspects of the counter-reformation are still with us. For example, there was the reform of church music, which paved the way to much of the polyphony that we now treasure. The training of the clergy was reformed too, with the establishment of seminaries in most Catholic dioceses.

So from one point of view the counter-reformation is the reform of the Roman Church from within as a belated response to the Reformation proper, and in religious terms it was a positive development. There is also the other counter-reformation which goes hand in hand with it. Some of the popes who were at the head of one counter-reformation were also at the head of the other counter-reformation – the attempt to win back the protestant countries to the unity of Christendom. To some extent this was attempted by missionary means, though rather more by military means. Sometimes, both approaches were used together.

Papal reaction to the protest had not always been so energetic. When Luther had published his 95 Theses, Rome's response had been lackadaisical in the extreme. One of the alleged responses of Pope Leo X was to observe, 'This Luther is a German. He must be a drunkard. He will feel better tomorrow when he has had a rest'.

The climate of the counter-reformation at least meant that papal reaction to the challenge of reform became more serious. John Bossy notes that as an institution the papacy, during the course of the sixteenth century, became an active force in a way that it had not been in the fifteenth century. For example, Pope Paul III, who was Pope from 1534 to 1549, was not an especially spiritual or devout man, but was adept at using the machinery of the papacy for governing the Church. Nearly all of the developments which came to characterise the counter-reformation were launched during his papacy. The Council of Trent began its work in 1545, responding to the need for reform perceived within the Church and to the challenge of the reformers. The Roman inquisition was relaunched under the Pope's authority in 1542. Both of these measures helped to oil the administrative machinery of papal government.

At first glance Paul III would not seem to be a likely candidate for a reforming pope. He was the last surviving cardinal from the clutch created by the notorious Borgia Pope, Alexander VI. But personal piety was not a papal requirement – that could come from elsewhere. Paul saw the need for reform and did not stand in the way of new ideas.

One of the new ideas was a very simple one. It came from a Basque soldier called Ignatius who read the gospels, underwent a conversion experience and felt called to travel to the Holy Land to live where Jesus had lived. This plan came to nothing, largely because the Franciscans, who were in charge of most of the Christian shrines in the Holy Land, were not keen on missionary newcomers. That setback was to be momentous for the Catholic Church. Ignatius, who was no academic, returned to Europe and spent several years at universities in Spain and France. His purpose, he said, was the study to save souls. Others were not so sure. His zeal attracted the suspicion of the Inquisition and he was accused of heresy at least twice.

But Ignatius was also a source of inspiration. In 1537 he and seven other like-minded friends, realising that Holy Land was an impossible goal, applied to the worldly Paul III offering their services. The process had begun which would give birth to the Society of Jesus – the Jesuits. The Catholic Church had many religious orders. Why did Ignatius and his followers have such an impact on his Church? Jack Scarisbrick, Professor of History at Warwick University, says that what was new about Ignatius was his idea that you found God in everything, and this is the keynote to his spirituality. You find God in the smallest leaf falling from a tree or the humblest worm in the ground, let alone the stars and planets in the heavens. And if you find God in everything then the need for prayer, which is simply opening your heart and mind to God, is correspondingly reduced.

Belief that God is to be found in everything also goes hand in hand with another hallmark of Jesuit spirituality – activism. The Jesuits aimed to get out and do things; to preach, to administer the sacraments and to proclaim the good news.

Ignatius' reputation would come to be very different. The man who told his followers to meet the challenge of protestant ideas with charity and without contempt, would in the end be thought of as 'the hammer of the heretics'. An unfair assessment, according to John Bossy, who believes that Luther and Ignatius, for all their intellectual and temperamental differences, had much in common. Both of them drew heavily on the extremely diverse and rather vigorous piety of the fifteenth and early sixteenth centuries. With Ignatius it shows in his desire that those who followed him should cultivate a vivid visual image of the life of Christ and incidents of His life that were relevant to their own situations. With Luther you get devotion to the person of Christ – in particular the suffering Christ – and to some extent the other aspects of the life of Christ, the nativity and babyhood. In general terms, therefore, there is a sense of the devotional importance of the humanity of Jesus.

Although intellectually Luther was far ahead of Ignatius, even on an educational level, they had something in common. However in the future the term 'Jesuit' would become synonymous with machiavellian plotting. Ignatius himself began from a very simple starting point. Father Philip Endean, a Jesuit from Campion Hall in Oxford, believes he was captivated by the Gospels. What is important about him is the fact that he – and Luther – had access to printed books and the printed accounts of the Gospel; they could read these printed books and could be converted by them, and that was a sixteenth century innovation, even for the very educated.

While Ignatius, the mature student, was pursuing his further education, grappling with Latin in Barcelona, a young girl with a taste for romantic literature, perfume and jewellery was growing up in a comfortable home in the Castilian town of Avila. At the age of twenty, against her

*Ignatius Loyola, the mystic ex-soldier and mature student who founded
the Jesuits, the most controversial of religious orders,
loved and hated by popes*

father's wishes, after reading the letters of St Jerome, she decided to become a nun in the local Carmelite convent.

This was not a place of religious fervour. The nuns were allowed to go off on holidays. They were allowed to wear high heels, padded dresses and coloured sashes. They could keep pets and servants and drank out of silver cups. They still spent time in chapel every day but the atmosphere of the convent was more like that of a hotel for the religiously inclined than a monastery.

Before long, Teresa abandoned the practice of private mental prayer. When her father died she began again and this time she persevered. As her spiritual life deepened, she became dissatisfied with the easy-going life around her at the Convent of the Incarnation and decided to leave to set up a new reformed Carmelite convent in 1562. What was different about the new convent of St Joseph in Avila and why did Teresa's reforms work? Shirley du Boulay, biographer of St Teresa, sees austerity allied to prayer as the keynote. It would not be everyone's idea of paradise, but it was Teresa's. She wanted poverty, silence and simplicity. She wanted the nuns to practise austerity and mortification, and she wanted them to spend long hours in solitude and prayer. Most of all, she wanted the convents to be places of love and she used to call St Joseph's – her first convent – her little dovecote.

She was aged 45 when she began her work of reformation – quite an elderly lady by the standards of her time – but there were at least two things which helped her. She was possessed of extraordinary charm and tact and could persuade people to do almost anything. If she could not get what she wanted direct, she would write. She would write to the provincial of the Carmelites, and she wrote to the King – Philip II – quite often, and she managed to win people over.

Secondly, she was very determined and this kept her going in the face of all sorts of opposition. Above and beyond both of these characteristics, however, she did believe in the voice of God, and she listened to it, although it often told her things that she did not want to hear. She knew what would happen if she started reforming the order, and she knew that there would be trouble ahead. Also, she probably felt in her bones that she was capable of more than she was doing.

Teresa knew she was part of a large movement pressing for reform within the Catholic Church. Some of her writings were examined by the Inquisition – she welcomed their interest – but she never fell foul of charges of heresy in the way Ignatius had.

In years to come the Jesuits would run into problems with several of the popes. Professor Scarisbrick says that everywhere the Jesuits went, they attracted intense admiration and equally fierce criticism, above all among their co-religionists, not just the protestants. From the start, Rome had a slightly ambivalent attitude. Religious orders are a mixed blessing, so far as popes are concerned, because they tend to be a law unto themselves. Ignatius had tried to placate this nervousness by adding a fourth vow to the usual three of poverty, chastity and obedience; the fourth vow was one of special, personal obedience to the Pope. Some popes welcomed this and used the Jesuits, but others kept them at arm's length. By the end of the seventeenth century it would be fair to say that most Jesuits looked to princes rather than popes for patronage. In particular, they allied themselves to the Bourbons.

This proved to be a fatal alliance, because the French royal family, the Bourbons, sold them down the river. When the time came for the convergence of their enemies, the Jesuits were attacked from all directions. They were expelled from France, from the Hapsburg colonies and from the Portuguese colonies. People were settling scores and, apart from the genuine religious objections and hostilities that undoubtedly existed, ultimately the Jesuits were sacrificed on the altar of European colonialism.

Teresa would meet no such difficulties. Her skill as a writer took her ideas all over the world. Even today her *Interior Castle* still holds its own as one of the classic descriptions of the mystical life. The worst Teresa's reputation had to suffer were some murmurings about her relationship with an intense young man called John of the Cross. Shirley du Boulay says any speculation about a romantic attachment between them is misplaced. She points out that John was only twenty five when they met; Teresa was fifty two. He was a Carmelite too and, like Teresa, was dissatisfied with the laxity of the life. Teresa immediately recognised his quality and persuaded him to become her first discalced or reformed Carmelite friar and founded a convent for him. They were friends and had a lot of respect for each other. She used to call him 'my little Seneca' and 'the father of my soul'. They were undoubtedly fond of each other. There are many stories about them which may be taken with a fairly liberal pinch of salt – for instance, about how they were meditating together and elevated up to the ceiling of the parlour in the Convent of the

Teresa of Avila (pictured here with John of the Cross), the reforming nun, once famed for her dimples, who inspired many by her writings on the spiritual life

Incarnation, chairs and all. Their personalities were, nevertheless, very different. She was lively and subjective and rather personal. He was objective and detached. She was a pragmatist, while he was a theoretical theologian. There was an interesting contrast – and overlap – in that she was almost masculine in her powers of leadership and in her determination, while he had an almost feminine sensitivity.

In Rome Paul III let it be known he wanted to call a Council to address the need for reform within the Catholic Church and to heal the divisions between Christians, not least so that Europe could present a united front to the Turks to discourage attack. The Council was convened at Trent and it achieved only limited reform. But with all the pressure for change, inside and outside the Catholic Church, why did it not achieve more? Peter Burke, Fellow of Emmanuel College, Cambridge says it is important not to underestimate the political pressures against reform or the manipulative powers of those in the Church who wanted to maintain the status quo. Those who were against reform shrewdly divided the opposition. There were three groups who wanted reform – the French, the Spanish and an Imperial party – but they wanted reform of different kinds. A deal was struck with the leader of each of the three groups – privately – and no Church-wide reform took place. In the empire, people were allowed to take communion either by drinking the wine or by taking bread, and the emperor Charles V stopped agitating for reform in consequence.

The French wanted a vernacular liturgy; they did not get that, but other concessions were made, and they stopped arguing too. The Spanish wanted more power for bishops, but all this was negotiable locally. As a political story, it is of considerable interest, because in 1562 and 1563, with so many bishops wanting reform, it must have looked as if this time the papacy was going to be out-voted. It had not been such a problem in 1545 and 1546 because of the 700 bishops eligible, only thirty or so turned up, giving the Italians a majority. But the challenge of 1562 and 1563 was quite another matter, and the papacy only got off the hook by dint of some very high class politicking. From another point of view, however, this was the great opportunity missed.

From the outset it had seemed unlikely that Trent would live up to the highest of papal hopes. Michael Walsh, says it was expected that Luther, or at least those who were in sympathy with his theology would attend, but they did not, except for one not very successful foray. The Vatican did not imagine that the schism would be permanent, and expected to resolve it. The man in charge of Luther's own religious order, the Augustinians, did put forward a theory on justification by faith which could, perhaps, have won back the Lutheran reformers, but it was opposed vigorously by a couple of Jesuits and was comprehensively squashed. Far from being a healer, the Council of Trent ended up by making the divisions between Christians sharper.

According to Peter Burke, many people think that the Reformation was simply Martin Luther saying something new, with people either springing to his defence or rallying to oppose him immediately, neatly dividing Europe into Catholics and Protestants in the process.

In fact, Luther did not know that he was a Protestant, and he certainly did not think that he was a Lutheran. There were some twenty to thirty years of ambiguity and, for better or worse, the function of the Council of Trent was to clear up these ambiguities. From then onwards, people knew exactly what they were; they were either Catholic or Protestant. Before Trent, everything was very far from being black and white. Take, for instance, the question of justification by faith. The text books will tell you that this was a Protestant doctrine and a litmus test for identifying Protestants from Catholics. Yet many of the Catholic clergy – including a number of bishops – who attended Trent believed in justification by faith until it was condemned in the final sessions of the Council. Then they had to make their decision. So the Council of Trent was a great definer, crystalliser and divider of Christendom.

One seventeenth-century historian remarked that, for him, the Council of Trent illustrated the great irony of history that the consequences of actions can be not just different from what was originally intended, but utterly opposite to what was originally intended. The Council was called in order to reunite Christendom; in the end, it divided it more sharply than before. It was called to reform the Church, but did nothing of the kind. It was called to reduce the power of the papacy and, in the end, extended it.

The Council of Trent dashed any hopes for an easy reunification of Christians but its effects were not entirely negative. In the short term it brought definition to Catholic belief. Protestant reformers had attacked the Eucharist saying it was merely a memorial of Christ; this provoked an emphasis on the Real Presence. Veneration of images, the value of processions and pilgrimages were all questioned by the Protestants and so after Trent they were all enthusiastically reaffirmed.

As John Bossy sees it, the long term effects of Trent and the counter-reformation as a whole were to resist a complete take over of western Christianity by the Protestant Reformation. They also modified the medieval devotional tradition, so that Catholicism could at least appear to compete on equal terms with the alternative versions of Christianity which developed from the Reformation.

After Trent, the Roman Church made a remarkable recovery indeed, to such an extent that it was able to exploit favourable developments in the outside world later on. Above all the Council of Trent set the tone for Catholic theological exploration and understanding of the papacy for centuries to come.

Peter Burke says that the effects of Trent were widespread. Some Catholic theologians had to distance themselves from thinking which had been perfectly acceptable before the Council. Also, the institutional power of the Pope had not only been reaffirmed, but increased. Before Trent and the Counter-Reformation, there had been considerable controversy over the political structure of the Church, and this echoed similar debates on the political structure of the secular state.

In the best classical tradition, three possible solutions were put forward. You could have a monarchy, an aristocracy or a democracy. A papal monarchy had many backers, but there were plenty of bishops and cardinals who thought they should also be consulted and so, predictably, favoured the aristocratic solution. A few people believed in the democratic model, with parish clergy being consulted – a few people thought that the laity should have some say too. It must be remembered that there were parts of Europe where parishioners elected the parish priest; this happened in Venice, for example. So it is by no means anachronistic or fanciful to say that there was a democratic tradition in the Catholic Church, so long as it is also remembered that it was a minority tradition. After Trent, however, this option was shut down, as was the aristocratic option. The Church became an absolute monarchy along the same lines as monarchies in France, Spain and elsewhere. Centralised government was also developing in secular Europe during the sixteenth century, and the Council of Trent encouraged this tendency in the Church as well.

The Catholic Church post-Trent also began to look increasingly beyond the confines of Europe. The time seemed right for mission. Ignatius's Jesuits were in the thick of it, going to South America, India,

Japan and China. Their method of mission work was controversial. They absorbed local culture and built on indigenous beliefs to prepare the way for Christianity – a slow method but the Italian Jesuit Matteo Ricci and his colleagues who went to China were nothing if not patient. Father Robert Murray SJ, Senior Research Fellow at Heythrop College, London, says that at first Ricci and his fellow Jesuits dressed as Buddhist monks. They opened a little chapel and they would encourage people to come in. The Chinese came in, sniffed the incense and stared at the statues. So far, so good – but could it be classified as teaching them about Christianity?

Ricci realised that, if he wanted to make any impact, he would have to master the language and master the Confucian classics – which were what the educated people lived by. He spent years in study. The Jesuits who had been in China before him were not as good at Chinese as Ricci was, but they had started trying to present items of the Christian faith in Chinese. They had translated the Ten Commandments and the Lord's Prayer, for example, but then they had begun a more ambitious exposition of the Christian faith. Ricci took this over and gradually built it up with the help of Chinese converts. That great work was called *The True Meaning of the Lord of Heaven*. The Lord of Heaven was the name they chose for God. In Chinese, the word for 'heaven' also means the sky or the weather. This was an expository work which built on all the elements in the Chinese classics which Ricci felt to represent good, natural religion. That was always the Jesuit method – to incorporate all the elements that were usable in native religions.

Jesuit missionary methods, criticised at the time, are only now receiving the recognition they deserve. Professor Jack Scarisbrick says that this insistence that Christianity must cease to be European if it was to become incarnate in China or Japan, India or North America, was the Jesuits' greatest contribution to missiology. The Jesuits believed that they had to cast off their European habit in order to enter into the hearts and minds of the people they were trying to convert. In China, for example, Ricci tried to find in Confucius the same kind of non-Christian basis upon which Christian revelation could rest as, in the Middle Ages, the Church in the West had found in Aristotle. Similarly, in Hinduism they tried to find what we would call the 'Hidden Christ'. In North America, they outraged the French authorities by saying that it was not necessary to become French or learn French in order to be a Christian.

*Matteo Ricci – linguist, sundial designer and clock maker extraordinary –
taking Christianity to China*

All of this may sound very obvious now, but given the ethnocentricity of the sixteenth-century European – witness the gusto with which the Spanish assaulted South American culture – the Jesuit approach was radically different. Indeed, it was revolutionary. It also contributed heavily to the suspicion with which many – inside the Church and out – regarded the Jesuits.

Nowhere was Jesuit missionary success more remarkable than in China. Matteo Ricci spent 28 years in China. When he began his work he came across no Chinese Christians yet when he died, he left behind a community of 2,500 believers. His was a Christian success story but there were those who said it was just a clockwork deception. Father Robert Murray explains that the Jesuits specialised in mechanical clocks and toys, things which the Chinese loved. Some said that this was merely an attempt to make clockwork 'rice' Christians. What it certainly did was to open up all sorts of cultural contacts which might otherwise have remained inaccessible. Through astronomy, the Jesuits were able to get almost to the heart of the imperial religion – because the calendar was of supreme importance. At the main feasts of the solstices and the equinoxes, the Emperor performed the rituals of the harmony of heaven and earth – what Blake used to call the marriage of heaven and earth in a different sense – and this had to be worked out absolutely accurately. Chinese astronomy was very good, but as the Chinese intellectuals came to know Ricci, they came to realise that western mathematics and astronomy were even better than their own. This gave the Jesuits tremendous prestige. Ricci's successors became the Astronomers Royal (or Imperial), and that continued even after Rome turned against the Jesuits' cultural methods.

Pressure from Rome became intense. It was said that Matteo Ricci had gone too far when he incorporated Chinese ancestor worship into Christian theology. Ricci was not helped by the difficulty of translating Chinese ideas. The Church had no difficulty in coping with veneration for saints or relics. Chinese reverence for their ancestors was interpreted as heathen worship. Matteo Ricci was disowned by Rome. It is only in the last fifty years that the injustice of that decision has been recognised.

Matteo Ricci was not the only Jesuit to be given a rough ride. Jesuits in England were regarded as potential regicides and many were put to death. On the continent Blaise Pascal, the great mystic, mathetician and theologian, laughed the Jesuits to scorn. Professor Scarisbrick says that Pascal was justified in pouncing on certain things that the Jesuits were saying and doing. They spent a lot of time hearing confession, and so concentrated on considering how to deal with particular cases of conscience. This was where they came to get their reputation for casuistry.

Broadly speaking, this meant the Jesuits always took the rather optimistic view that unless you could *prove* that something was wrong, it was quite all right to go ahead and do it. There was no single source which outlined what was right and what was wrong, so they relied on Jesuit authorities. Some Jesuit moral tracts demonstrated a stopwatch morality, saying that a certain action could be pursued up to a point, but no further. They taught that an action which was almost certain to lead to a transgression of the moral law, but which was not in itself sinful, was permitted. Pascal pounced on some of the more dubious bits of advice, lumped them together and then edited the result in a way which was less than entirely fair. This produced a brilliant book called *The Provincial Letters* which is supposed to be the letters exchanged with a Jesuit provincial. It is full of mock irony, with the writer saying, 'I am so delighted to read the Jesuit manuals because I now discover that I can do all the things that I thought I could not and, Father, I am so grateful.'

Pascal really sent up the Jesuits, and it did a lot of harm to their reputation. They never found an adequate way of replying to his attacks, and Pascal in effect coined the idea of the Jesuits being synonymous with scheming. But the Jesuits have always made enemies. They were accused of being king-killers by some, and of being divine rightists by others. You could always find some sort of stick with which to beat the Jesuits.

The sixteenth century in the Catholic Church not only formalised dogma, launched mission and shaped the papacy. Even those who were not in the thick of Church politics or were attached to the great reforming orders would notice changes. The message, if not the writing, was on the wall. Peter Burke points out that the iconography of the interior decoration of churches changed dramatically after the Council of Trent, and in a Tridentine direction. If one makes a study of the images most frequently represented on the walls and ceilings of churches in the baroque period – which is the period after the Council of Trent – you will constantly find images which represent the doctrines which the Protestants challenged.

Even in art, Catholics are constantly arguing with the invisible Protestants, on the walls and ceilings of their churches. Some say that it was a subliminal response to the Protestant challenge, and that it was mounted in this way because those in power in the Catholic Church thought it was better not to argue outright with the Protestants, because that would entail Catholics discovering what Protestants thought, and – you never knew – they might be attracted by it. But if, instead, you presented these images, then the minds of the faithful would be led in the right direction. However conscious that policy was, the result cannot be ignored. The effect of the Council of Trent on art is certainly the most accessible to us in the late twentieth century.

In the end 'counter-reformation' does not fully describe what went on in the Catholic Church in the sixteenth century. To put it in human terms, if Ignatius of Loyola and Martin Luther had ever met, would they have found themselves diametrically opposed to one another? Father Philip Endean says that for all the debate about reformation, Catholic reform and counter-reformation, it might be more useful to think in terms of the 'formation' rather than the 'reformation'. He points out that what was going on in the sixteenth century in Europe was a far-reaching set of social and cultural changes, bound up with the discovery of the New World, the rediscovery of the pagan classics and the invention of printing. These discoveries brought about a complete transformation of people's sense of who they were. Inevitably, this had its effect on religion, and if you see Ignatius and Luther, the Protestant reformers and the Catholic reformers, as part of the same phenomenon, you are getting much closer to the truth.

CHAPTER V

AN ALTERNATIVE
TO TOBACCO

'Now I saw in my dream that at the end of this valley lay blood, bones, ashes and the mangled bodies of men; and while I was musing what should be the reason I espied, a little before me, a cave, where two giants Pope and Pagan, dwelt in old time, by whose power and tyranny the men whose blood, bones and ashes lay there, were cruelly put to death . . . But I have learnt since that Pagan has been dead many a day; as for the other, though he be yet alive, he is by reason of age, grown so crazy and stiff in his joints that he now can do little more than sit in his cave's mouth grinning at pilgrims as they go by, biting his nails because he cannot come at them.'

Words written by John Bunyan, the tinker's son who was to spend twelve years of his life in prison for his uncomfortably powerful preaching.

There are many odd beliefs about the history of the quarrelling Christian family. One of the least well founded is the assumption that after the fire of Martin Luther and the fury of Henry VIII, and after measured and unmeasured responses from Rome, religious hackles were relaxed and a calm and unquestioning climate prevailed over the newly-divided Christian world.

Nothing could be further from the truth. The seventeenth century and the early eighteenth century was a time when religious tides and cross tides were strong. It was a time of tremendous energy, of visions and hatreds, of independence and narrow-mindedness, of new beginnings and promised lands.

In this chapter we will forget about popes and princes, about dynastic fears and reform imposed from above. We concentrate on a tinker's son, an apprentice cobbler and a five foot three charismatic preacher who would sway crowds but suffered at the hands of his wife who used to drag him across the floor by his hair. We will also pay attention to people's language and discover the bellicose roots of some pacifists and also find out how seventeenth-century reformers still exercise an unexpected influence over the power politics of our secular world today.

But first of all, let us get our stereotypes straight. The seventeenth century was the heyday of the Puritans, those ardent Protestants who wanted no truck with Rome or the Romish past. They are sometimes identified as the killjoys of 'Merrie England'. But Professor Patrick Collinson says that 'Merrie England' was something which was supposed to be dying throughout its history. The phrase really came from people saying at the time of the Reformation, 'It was never a merry world since we had all this preaching amongst us' and so on. There was a feeling on all sides that the kind of merriment and socially relaxed ways of the past were disappearing. That was partly mythical. There is always a kind of myth about the good old times, and the changes of the Reformation served to underline it.

But the Puritans and others were certainly concerned about limiting the number of alehouses. There was a lot of concern about what you might call the alehouse culture and people mis-spending their money and time in alehouses. There was anxiety about drink – although the seventeenth-century Puritans were not teetotalers – and there was also worry about Sabbath abuse, including the buying and selling of fruit and vegetables on Sundays generally, and dancing and football on Sunday afternoons. There was great anxiety about football in particular, which at the time was a very violent game in which people were quite often killed. There was concern about youthful sexuality, and particularly its expression in dancing. This kind of problem boiled up afresh every Sunday, when there would be a tremendous struggle over how Sunday was to be observed.

There were also more seasonal things like maypoles and great antipathy to the whole May festival with its phallic symbols and all the other carryings-on that were generally assumed to take place at that time. In addition there were the local church fundraising efforts which could involve bullbaiting, dancing and a certain amount of rowdy behaviour. The Puritans and other worthy figures in the community were all in favour of raising money, but by rational means – that is by rating the inhabitants and collecting money from them officially rather than through their having a good time. All this led to a great deal of cultural tension and conflict.

Many Puritans felt that the Reformation in England had been left half-finished. Some among them questioned the need for bishops – the mitre was more of a sign of Satan than of Christ, they said. James I was in no mood to grant any concessions. He knew that if the authority of the bishops was questioned, before long, a king might be threatened too. The majority of Puritans stayed in England but some, now known as the Pilgrims, or the Pilgrim Fathers, set sail for a new promised land. Professor Richard Marius, head of the Expository Writing Program at Harvard College, describes the Pilgrims as being several different groups of people who had in common the fact that they hated bishops and set out to America to set up their own congregational system of government so that they could be immune from the Thirty-Nine Articles and the corruption, as they saw it, of the Anglican Church. Originally they set off for Virginia, but they were blown off course and landed in Massachusetts in 1620, where they had a very hard time initially. However, by 1630 there were quite a number of Puritan settlements all around Massachusetts. They were Calvinists and they believed in predestination, but the most important thing is their strong belief in congregational government.

Those principles and particularly the emphasis on congregational government were destined to have a profound effect on the development of America. Puritans, in England and America, wanted a complete Protestant reformation and were unhappy about old ways – even down to everyday language. Patrick Collinson says that their speech was probably recognisably different – a godly speech characterised chiefly by the fact that they did not swear. One could almost have divided the population of England into swearers and non-swearers. There were no Protestant oaths. If you wanted to swear, it had to be in Catholic language, as it were. Those who said 'By the Mass' or 'By God's body' or 'By God's wounds', or used the term 'bloody' ('By Our Lady') proclaimed the fact that they were not good Protestants. The Puritans did not swear and reprehended those who did.

That tendency to reprove did not add to Puritan popularity in the non-Puritan part of the population. Puritans were thought of as interferers, and were spoken of without affection as 'busy controllers'. James I had had no time for their presbyterian ideas. When Charles I came to the throne in 1625, the Puritans found themselves even more out of favour and feared that the new king and William Laud, the Archbishop of

Canterbury, were preparing to sell the Protestant pass. Clare Cross, Professor of History at York University, points out that Charles I executed a complete U-turn as far as the Calvinist sympathies of his father James I were concerned. Charles patronised a new faction in the English Church which was promoting a new idea of that Church which was neither fully Protestant nor, of course, Roman Catholic, but which emphasised the sacraments as against sermons. The followers of Archbishop Laud recreated or redefined Puritanism. By the time of the coming of Laud, men and women who had thought of themselves as perfectly orthodox members of the English Church were being branded as Puritans. Naturally they became very indignant about this.

Therefore by the time of the Civil War in 1642, when Laud was thrust out of power and finally put to death, this body of people with Puritan sympathies wanted to reassert what they saw as the 'orthodox' tradition of the Church of England. Then the problem arose about what sort of Church they wanted to create. There was a tension between the ruling classes in general, who were represented in Parliament, and the Army. In the Army there tended to be the sort of Protestantism that favoured local churches and the independence of local congregations and which did not want a tightly disciplined state Church. Inevitably this brought it into conflict with the 'orthodox' faction represented in Parliament.

In some ways the Puritans were at odds with their society, but in other ways they were more representative of their time than we might think. Patrick Collinson points out that there was widespread and intense moral sensitivity, which was not the sole prerogative of the Puritans. According to our standards today we should have found the moral attitudes of almost everyone in those times to have been Puritan. For example, in Colchester, Essex, fornicators and adulterers were put into a tumbril and carted round the streets in a curious species of shaming ritual, almost a mock wedding. The guilty couple stood up in the cart with big placards round their necks proclaiming that they had committed adultery (you can still see some of these placards in Colchester Museum).

This was not merely a Puritan affair. Everybody approved. That was just what you did with people who transgressed sexually. True, some of the Colchester Puritans favoured a long route for the cart rather than a short one, and wanted the punishment administered in some cases where the evidence was not all that strong – in other words, they were slightly over-enthusiastic but the whole process was something which most

Some of the Pilgrim Fathers, whose congregational ecclesiology still moulds American politics today, about to set sail to their Promised Land

Printed for Nat: Ponder on the Poultry

John Bunyan, the tinker's son, who wrote 'Pilgrim's Progress', the greatest spiritual allegory in the English language which also packs an often ignored political punch

people agreed with.

From 1642, everyone in England would have their worlds turned inside out by the Civil War. John Bunyan, the tinker's son, who would write the greatest allegory in the English language, was a beneficiary of army life. Christopher Hill, former master of Balliol College, Oxford, is convinced that Bunyan received his education while he was in the army. He says Bunyan was in the Parliamentary army for two and a half years, from the age of sixteen to eighteen and a half. The war was going on for only six out of those eighteen months and armies, when they have to sit about after a war is over tend to do nothing but talk and they usually become pretty bolshy. There is no doubt that Bunyan came up against plenty of very wild radical talk in the army. We know in particular that there was great dissent at Newport Pagnell, the garrison town where he was stationed. The correspondence of the commanding officer there shows he was horrified at the things his troops were saying and doing. In *Grace Abounding*, his religious autobiography, Bunyan tells of the struggle he had with the devil, who tried to destroy his faith – and the devil uses all the arguments which we know the radicals were using in the Army.

There was a group called the Ranters who said that if you are satisfied in your own conscience that what you are doing is right, then to hell with the Bible, to hell with the Lord and to hell with everything else, your conscience is the only thing that matters. They said, incidentally, that their consciences told them to sleep with as many women as they could, and Bunyan said that he found that rather attractive – 'I being a young man and my nature at its prime'. It is fairly clear that when he came out of the army and came back to his village he was a wide boy, as you might say, and took the lead among the hooligans of the village. His best friend, he says, was a permanent drunk, and he himself used to drink but he says he remained chaste.

For two or three years after he came out of the army, Bunyan was unsettled. No religious answers satisfied him until he came across a group of women sitting on their doorsteps in the sun and talking about the things of God as he put it 'as if joy did make them speak'. He listened to them, asked to be put in contact with their congregation and before long was their star preacher. His fame spread quickly. His radical views in support of the poor gained him powerful enemies and prison sentences, but still he continued preaching and writing.

While Bunyan was in the army, one of his contemporaries, a failed shoe-maker, was wandering through the country, interrupting church services and arguing about Christianity with everyone. That man was George Fox, remembered now as the founding father of Quakerism. Jonathan Fryer, his biographer, describes him as a fairly lithe and fit young man in his early years – as he needed to be for the sort of lifestyle that he had. Many people were impressed by his striking looks, in particular his fierce eyes – in the records concerning him it is quite a common thing to find people more or less running away from him, saying, 'Get that man away from me – he must not look at me.' Of course this was a period when witchcraft was still very much alive in England, and Fox travelled around Pendle Hill, one of the great centres of witch-craft. Some people did believe he was a witch, which could very easily have lost him his life. He wore his hair very long and refused to powder it or to wear any of the ribbons and decorations that were fashionable before the Parliamentary period. One of his most famous eccentricities was to dress in a leather suit, which caused considerable comment.

Both Bunyan and Fox were seen as threats to the established church. After the Civil War there is a change of language. 'Puritan' appears less frequently and 'non-conformist' takes its place. The name has changed but the pre-occupations and the desire to turn to a simple Christianity remain. There is a further twist to the tale which intensified religious enthusiasms. Christopher Hill explains that there had been a great revol-ution which had overthrown all the traditional things like Church and King – and when you've finally chopped a King's head off there's not really much further you can go. Bishops had been abolished too; every-thing was topsy-turvy. Some people actually believed that after Charles I the next king would be King Jesus, because they were sure that the end of the world was coming. Millenarianism was in the air. It had been ex-ploited by Parliamentarian propaganda in the Civil War, because per-suading people to fight against the King at all was a difficult job in terms of the traditional values. The only cause greater than the King's could be God's cause – so the Parliamentarians had to be fighting for God's cause.

Today we think that people who believe that the end of the world is coming are barmy but by the end of the seventeenth century many books had been published by biblical scholars concentrating on the Book of Daniel and the Book of Revelations and other parts of the Bible where there are hints about when the end of the world is going to be. All the best experts of the seventeenth century believed that the biblical evidence suggested that either the end of the world itself, or a very marked step towards it, was going to come in the middle of the seventeenth century. All this, remember, is not the work of a lunatic fringe, but of the best mathematicians, ancient historians and chronologers in the country. John Napier, the inventor of logarithms, used them to work out the significance of the number 666, which was one of the key elements, and at the end of the century Isaac Newton was still working out when the end of the world was coming with the aid of the higher mathematics. It was a serious academic subject.

After the Civil War, non-conformists suffered from intermittant persecution and consistent mockery. 'You people are the tremblers, you are quakers,' a judge told Fox at the blasphemy trial of one of his followers. Fox's disillusionment with the established church had not been helped by the useless advice which had been handed out to him earlier by clergymen. When he put his religious questions to one parson, he was advised to take up tobacco. But many people took Fox more seriously. He was an outstanding speaker but one who could also keep quiet.

Jonathan Fryer describes how he would stand on a rock outside the church. He loved preaching in the churchyards in the hope of winkling the congregation out of the building to come and listen to him instead. He would speak for three or four hours in a great tirade which he believed would open up the truth to people. There was one marvellous occasion which he recorded in his journal, when thousands of his followers went to a great meeting, out in the fields in the north of England on a fine summer's day, to hear him speak. He arrived there and suddenly became conscious of an extraordinary atmosphere. He realized that he did not need to say anything because the spirit of God and the light of Christ were there and the people could concentrate on that. Increasingly over the next few years Quaker meetings became silent, or at least based on silence. They became an occasion when friends came together to sit, not just doing nothing, but rather preparing themselves in the silence and waiting on the spirit of the Lord.

Quakers believe that the spirit of the Lord will move certain people to say something – or even move people to say nothing – but whatever happens, everything that is said should come from impulse. This brings us back to the reason why Fox's followers were called Quakers: today, still, at Quaker meetings you can find people who begin to tremble and quake, and when they stand up what they have to say does come out almost as if someone were speaking through them rather than that they are speaking themselves.

Like Bunyan, George Fox would become familiar with the insides of prisons. The restoration of the monarchy was not good news for puritan non-conformists. Clare Cross explains how the reign of Charles II witnessed the great period of persecution of Puritans. There is a tendency to blame this on Charles himself but he had his own reasons for wanting toleration towards all sorts of Protestants – he wanted toleration of Catholics. But Parliament from 1662 onwards was frightened of the political threat which they saw in the stricter sorts of Protestant sects, and the members of Parliament were the people who initiated the persecutions.

This can be seen very easily – to put it simply, when Parliament was in session there was persecution of those who refused to go to the Church of England services, and when it was not in session there was much more toleration. But there was no official toleration until James II was thrown out and William and Mary came to the throne. Even then it was only a very grudging toleration of Protestants who did not subscribe to the Church of England. They were allowed to meet in their meeting-houses, but only so long as the doors were open. They were really second-class citizens and they were debarred from holding office in local or national government or going to the universities until the coming of the nineteenth century.

The establishment did not have everything its own way. George Fox was a force for change, but then he and his followers were not above change themselves. In the 1650s Fox was all for Oliver Cromwell taking up arms against the Pope – one Quaker soldier was as good as seven non-Quaker soldiers, he said. But once Charles II was restored, the Quakers changed their warlike tune. After the restoration of Charles II there was obvious consternation among all the radicals. Most of them had the sense to see that the game was up. The swing of the men of property in the opposite direction to theirs was so overwhelming that there was nothing they could do about it.

There was one notable exception. A small group of the sect known as the Fifth Monarchists organized a revolt in January 1661 in London which terrorized the city for several days and was put down only with

George Fox, the founder of the Quakers who caused a stir with his theology, his fierce eyes and his refusal to powder his hair

tremendous difficulty. There were very few people involved in it but they fought with enormous courage. They believed God was going to intervene and were obviously rather disappointed when no miracle happened. As a result of this revolt there were widespread arrests of radicals. This included anyone suspected of being anti-Government, so Quakers in particular were in danger because of their rhetoric against the restoration of the monarchy.

Within ten days of the Fifth Monarchist revolt the Quakers published the Peace Principle which was a statement to the effect that they did not want to use carnal weapons in order to achieve political results. They were, they said, only interested in being left alone in their religion. From that day onwards this has been the official policy of the Quakers.

It took quite a struggle to impose it and there had to be a great enforcement of discipline in the movement, because otherwise people claiming to be Quakers were set to take action which the leadership did not approve of. It was a particularly acute problem because of the Quaker enthusiasm for doing things 'for a sign' – sensational things like going around naked. Under Fox discipline was established, slowly and rather painfully. It took a long time. Quakers were certainly taking part in plots to overthrow the Government by violence in the 1660s; several of them took part in the Northern Plot in 1663; and even in 1685, when the Duke of Monmouth tried to overthrow James II, several Quakers fought for him, and two of them were executed.

Even then, the Peace Principle had not been accepted by all those who called themselves Quakers. But once it had been finally established when the Quakers reprinted books and pamphlets, they took care not to reprint those that had advocated a Protestant crusade on the Continent. They edited out the more bellicose sentiments and in this way the bellicosity of the 1650s disappeared even from the historical record which the Quakers themselves built up. George Fox's own journal was very carefully edited, first of all by him and then, after he died, by others, who rather naively said that they did not wish anything to be left out which ought not to be left out or anything to be left in which ought not to be left in. Clearly they went through it with a blue pencil.

George Fox's writings were highly influential but the outstanding non-conformist writer of the seventeenth century has to be John Bunyan. His *Pilgrim's Progress*, an allegory of Bunyan's own religious struggle, has long been recognised as one of the landmarks of English Literature.

But it is also more than pious fable or beautiful prose. Christopher Hill says that there is of course no doubt that *Pilgrim's Progress* is about how you get to the celestial city, but on the way you meet people from different classes and it is pretty clear which side Bunyan is on. The giants and monsters he meets are all gentlemen, all landlords. They say, 'What are you doing on my ground.' The giants and monsters are enclosing even the King's highway, which is of course just what people were doing in the seventeenth century. Not only were the giants enclosing landlords but they had jurisdictional rights to and could detain the pilgrims in a private lockup. In a word, they were Justices of the Peace, as most enclosers were in the seventeenth century. It is perfectly clear to contemporary readers that the baddies all belonged to the ruling-class.

Pilgrim's Progress and *Grace Abounding*, Bunyan's autobiography, were to have a profound influence on non-conformist thinking. The keen awareness of social injustice felt by Fox and Bunyan would soon find a new, powerful advocate. John Wesley, born in 1703, did not come from such a grindingly poor background as they had done, but he still had problems to overcome. The Reverend Henry Rack, biographer of Wesley and lecturer at Manchester University, points out that the Wesley family was unusual. There are supposed to have been about nineteen children, (his mother was one of twenty-four or possibly twenty-five – her father was not sure) of whom about eight survived: three boys, Samuel junior, John, and Charles the hymn-writer, and five very intelligent girls, who made dreadfully unhappy marriages. Many people think John was dominated by his mother. One wonders whether his mother did perhaps ruin his capacity for relationships with women by the tremendous discipline which she instilled into him, and the others. He had several very affectionate love affairs, but he was so hesitant about proposing and so entangled with the thought that he probably ought to be celibate that twice he made a complete mess of it. Another party stepped in, and got the girl. Finally, at the age about 45, he married and it was an absolute disaster. There are all sorts of stories about his wife, including the one about how she dragged him around the room by his hair – he was a very small man, about five foot three-and-a-half and quite slight, so it must have been fairly easy. She scolded him like a fishwife and accused him of adultery with his female correspondents. It was a very unhappy story.

Despite the Wesleys' lack of money, John and his brother Charles had been given excellent educations. After a scholarship to the Charterhouse,

John went off to Oxford and there began to live a holy life, methodically marking his success or failure on a scale from one to ten. From Oxford he went to Georgia as a missionary. But it is a mistake to think of America solely as a mission field. Wesley's American contemporary, Jonathan Edwards, would preside over a religious revival known as 'The Great Awakening'. This would affect both sides of the Atlantic, but it began with a simple sermon. Dr Bob Bliss, lecturer in American history at Lancaster University, tells how Edwards preached an awakening message, a warning 'election' sermon saying that New England was backsliding from Calvinism and the creeds of the seventeenth century. Then around 1734–5, he began to notice how people were laid low with anxiety and depression, depending too much on the creaturely world and not enough on the Spirit and failing to realise that it was God's power and not man's that would determine their salvation. He kept on preaching and people of all kinds began to take his words to heart. He acquired a vision of a new social peace – a vision that perhaps America would be the place where the second coming of God's kingdom would be seen. Some historians have seen this as the beginning of the American conception of nationality, the American sacralising of the landscape and the American idea of a manifest destiny.

On both sides of the Atlantic the principle vehicle for religious revival was the sermon. When Wesley returned to England he had a religious experience which convinced him his life's work must be to preach the Christian message. This decision was to have startling results. People in the crowds listening to him screamed, turned black and red in the face, and fainted.

Henry Rack says that Wesley would not have been exciting to look at. All the congregation would have seen was a little man dressed carefully in, apparently, clerical garb – dark suit, plain clothes, gown, bands. But he certainly must have been very charismatic in some way. It is hard to get a flavour of this from reading his sermons in print, because they are a kind of carefully numbered skeleton outlines. Obviously, he must have delivered them in a very impassioned way – there are accounts of his working up to a climax with a tremendous piercing challenge. In some cases there were convulsions among his audience. There are also personal accounts by people who said, 'I thought his eye was on me, and that these words were directed especially at me.' It was a recurrent theme among his converts but it can hardly be objective, since there could have been easily two thousand people at a sermon. Afterwards people would be stirred to go up and see him personally, or write to him. Sometimes there was a form of mass hysteria but the deeper and more personal things did happen too. Sometimes, particularly in the early years, he was mobbed. There are dramatic accounts of hostile crowds more or less taking over, and of miraculous escapes – sometimes with the mob leader suddenly stopped dead in his tracks with club upraised, sometimes with Wesley even ending up being protected by the leader, or getting away with just a torn coat or a grazed elbow.

Wesley was by no means the only great preacher. George Whitefield could also draw the crowds. It was claimed that his first sermon drove fifteen people mad. Whitefield preached on both sides of the Atlantic. In America the 'Great Awakening' was exercising more than religious influence. Many believe it was the precursor to the American Revolution.

Bob Bliss says that there is a well-established line of argument about the connections between the Calvinist awakening and the Revolution. It is in part a question of giving to previously disenfranchised Calvinists, relatively powerless people on the lower end of the social scale, a sense of their own moral worth and moral autonomy, plus a certain amount of experience in fighting the Establishment – including law-breaking, political agitation and political action – to secure the fruits of the revival, like new churches and changes in the law about itinerant preachers. As a result, when the imperial crisis came, with its contemporaneous economic difficulties in the colonies, the colonists had a sense of their own virtue, and their right and ability to engage in political action. It has been argued that the enlightened elite of the colonies perceived this and often cast their message deliberately in Calvinist revivalistic terms; even Tom Paine said, 'If we don't throw the British out, we shall be guilty of a national sin.'

England was about to face its own revolution – the industrial revolution – which would transform the world which Bunyan, Fox and Wesley had been born into. Wesley has been accused of providing docile, self-improving factory fodder and white-washing capitalism – an unfair assessment according to Henry Rack who points out that Wesley's most famous sermon in this area was on the use of money. He says, 'Gain all you can, save all you can, give all you can,' – a classical three-point sermon. The real punch line lies in point three. In his old age nobody was ruder about the Methodists than Wesley himself. He would say, 'Here is one of life's ironies: by discipline of religion you have become frugal so you have done well and become rich, and now your souls are in danger – you don't get up for the early preaching and Methodism will collapse if we don't have early preaching.'

He went on and on about wealth in his old age, and extravagance in dress. He once asked, 'Shouldn't I have set up a uniform like the Quakers?' There were quite a few Quaker touches in his whole attitude to this subject in general. He was not really a supporter of the ruthless entrepreneur, but more of a supporter of the frugal small businessman. He was against conspicuous expenditure and said you could dress according to your station but it should be plain – not, he said, like those Quakers who dress in dark clothes but of the very best cloth.

The influence of the Puritans should not be underestimated. Like the Pilgrim Fathers, many Americans still believe their country is the promised land. Furthermore, Richard Marius believes the Puritans hold the key to many Americans' heartfelt beliefs about their own constitution.

American Puritanism founded the notion that the congregation, the assembly, should govern itself. People tired of the Puritans in less than a hundred years, because the standard of living in the colonies, and then the United States, quickly rose to be much higher for the average person than in Britain. And thus people began coming to New England and other colonies simply for the usual reason – to get a better life.

But there persisted the idea that a republican form of government, in which the whole group is represented by a council, or legislature, has as its function speaking for the whole assembly according to the ideas of right and wrong set out in the Puritan constitution – the Bible.

That notion carried over into American politics and to this very day the attitude in the United States towards the written constitution, which appears so strange to the people of Britain, is an attitude of the sacredness of the text of the written constitution, and the notion that the councils of the Republic, the Legislature and the Supreme Court are always interpreting that sacred text to find out how it applies today.

There is a real relation between this and the Puritan idea of the sacredness of the biblical text, and many underlying American political attitudes become understandable to the outsider only in terms of the Puritan element in the development of the United States. The Puritans were as positive in setting a direction towards true representative government as they were negative in their moralism, their self-righteousness, and their intolerance.

Chapter VI

Enthusiasts and a New Goddess

'Religion is nothing but stupidity. A true republican has no truck with superstition. He does not revere idols. His worship is reserved for liberty alone.'

'Pay homage to Reason, worship the Supreme Being, respect the law.'

Two conflicting voices from the French Revolution

The French Revolution was a feast of idealism and brutishness which attempted to outlaw Christianity and in its place enshrine the goddess Reason. It may seem fanciful to claim the French Revolution as part of the continuing process of religious reformation but if so, it is an old fancy. The nineteenth-century statesman and historian Alexis de Tocqueville described his country's revolution as a movement which had all the qualities of a religious revival barring a belief in God or in life after death. Too often the events of 1789 are dissected in glorious secular isolation. The revolution was more than a political adventure – it was part of the groundwell of essentially religious ideas, sweeping over the new and old worlds in the last half of the eighteenth century and the first half of the nineteenth.

This is the time when religious revival became synonymous with awakened social conscience, when Christians became dangerous, when they questioned the justification of slavery and child labour. It was also a time of controversy. This was the heyday of the missionary, long before the slur of imperialism had been thought of. This was also the time when opportunities began to open up for women to be active as well as praying Christians.

Revolution was in the air. As usual it depended on individuals. We shall meet an evangelical countess, some saints from Clapham, a cobbler turned linguist and an internationally famous missionary who only ever gained one convert but single-handedly changed the history of an entire continent. In the process we shall observe pub signs, the development of pressure group politics and the unwelcome birth of some pernicious prejudices.

But first we shall move with caution. In 1784 John Wesley agreed to the deed of declaration providing for his successors. From then on it was inevitable that Methodism would continue to exist as a movement in its own right, distinct from the established church. Methodists were still regarded with a degree of suspicion. Dr Donald English, former president of the Methodist Conference of Great Britain, makes the point that the civil wars in the seventeenth century had been largely about religion. Therefore, the eighteenth century was very nervous about what it called 'enthusiasm' – what we should call fanaticism. Someone going round the country doing what was called 'field preaching' – open-air preaching to large crowds of ordinary people – was looked upon by church leaders and some politicians as extremely dangerous. Also it has to be remembered that the French Revolution was looming, and people were aware that the same sort of thing could happen in Britain.

Religious revival in Britain was not confined to Wesley and his followers. The outstanding preacher of the age, George Whitefield, spearheaded the Calvinist mission. He found an ardent supporter in Selina, Countess of Huntingdon, who provided openings for revivalist or evangelical preachers to reach the aristocracy. When clergymen were banned from churches for their outspoken views, she would find them alternative pulpits either in chapels or in private homes. These non-conformist gatherings became known as 'the Countess of Huntingdon Connection'. Given that Whitefield is generally recognised as being a greater preacher than Wesley, why has his influence petered out? Clive Calver, director of the Evangelical Alliance, thinks that Whitefield's primary legacy lay, precisely, in the Countess of Huntingdon's Connection – and it was not the success that the Methodist churches were. The Connection was a loose association of churches (which still exists today) but Whitefield lacked Wesley's strategic grasp: Whitefield was a preacher, but not an organiser. He left behind nothing like Wesley's system of class meetings, training and stewards, with all their capacity to draw people together; what he bequeathed was chiefly the memory and the record of his preaching.

*John Wesley, the founder of Methodism, in old age contemplating the
gravestones of his remarkable mother, Susannah*

*Selina, Countess of Huntingdon – a lady with connections who
provided pulpits for outspoken preachers*

Whitefield's preaching was memorable but more than that, his message was disturbing. He criticised those members of the clergy who in his eyes were more bothered about hunting foxes than saving souls. He wanted to replace the comfortable secularism of the state church with an awakened understanding of the Gospels. Such enthusiasm was dangerous. In the years after his death, leading up to and through the French Revolution, all those in positions of privilege in the church had every reason to feel nervous. They had only to look over the Channel to see what new ideas could do to a once unassailable Church. Dom Aidan Bellenger, Benedictine monk and headmaster of Downside School, explains how before the French Revolution the Church in France was unified and national, self-confident, rich and well-managed, in complete charge of education and social service. In a way, it was seen as leading the nation to God under the King – the King being the great provider. After the Revolution the Church reflected only a part of French society – sometimes, perhaps, as much as half, sometimes much less. French society never again had the unity of faith which it had had before the Revolution; it became a pluralist society. The division in French society – monarchist and religious on the one side, republican and free-thinking on the other – was created from, roughly, the 1780s to the 1880s. It was a total transformation, a split down the middle which is still reflected to this day in French society between extreme right and extreme left. The Church, which had once been politically neutral, was, as a result of the Revolution, politicised.

The French Revolution induced an atmosphere of alarm. In such a climate of fear, Methodism could easily be seen as subversive by those in power. As Donald English says, it all had to do with doctrine. Wesley was not a Calvinist holding to doctrines of election – that those who are saved are those who are chosen to be saved. He was what was called an Arminian (from the name of the Dutch theologian Arminius, who believed that wherever the Gospel was preached all who heard could respond if they so chose). Thus Wesley's brother Charles could write in one hymn, 'For all, for all my Saviour died, for all, for all was crucified,' and that is reflected in the preaching. Wesley genuinely believed that all who heard him could respond and be saved. Of course this had political overtones too, because if you believe in God's love for all through Christ then you believe in the very best for all socially and politically as well.

The final years of the eighteenth century saw many new religious and political ideas. Words gained new meaning. Aidan Bellenger explains how the very word 'revolution' changed its meaning during this period, from meaning planets going round the sun to referring to violent political change. At the beginning of the Revolution, many of members of the Church in France, both bishops and lesser clergy, were in favour of change, but as time went on the Revolution and the Church became separated. The crucial moment came in 1790 with the Civil Constitution of the Clergy. The National Assembly, which had attempted to produce for France a very liberal constitution influenced by both English and American ideas, tried to bring the Church within that constitution and make it a part of the State. A great majority of both bishops and priests were not prepared to accept this. When the Civil Constitution oath was required in 1781 more than half the French clergy refused to take it and the French Church was split between the constitutionalists and the non-jurors, who became a kind of underground Church and a Church in exile, since after this point there were many clerical refugees.

In England the presence of French exiles increased awareness of the fragility of the establishment. Stories of the new regime's attempts to promulgate either atheism or a vague worship of the state, complete with sacred oaths and altars, did little to reassure the Church in England. John Briggs, director of the Victorian Studies Centre at the University of Keele, says that by the beginning of the nineteenth century there was a very real fear that the Church was in danger – the phrase was even adopted in one case as the sign of a pub. The danger was that the Church would be associated with the outdated part of society. The new towns appearing were largely unchurched; after the Napoleonic Wars Parliament passed two acts granting money for new church building in urban centres precisely because they thought an unchurched population would be a dangerous one. Officially, this was a thanksgiving for deliverance from Napoleon, but in actual fact it was a kind of insurance policy against civil unrest.

The establishment felt under threat. In its eyes the very type of people attracted to Methodism was a source of unease. As Donald English says, they were largely artisans; not the poorest of the poor but tradesmen, shoemakers, chairmakers, soldiers, teachers – the sort of people who in the normal scheme of things would not be allowed to express their opinions. The Church of England was very hierarchical, and so was the political system – one MP had forty relatives who were all MPs. But in the Methodist system, once you had responded to the Gospel you were gathered into the Methodist classes where your opinions were not ignored or just allowed but positively required. John Wesley had produced a set of questions which his classes had to answer and ordinary people who were beginning to feel themselves a group in the nation found this way of expressing not only their faith but their political and social interests – hence the close traditional link between Methodism and trade unionism.

Even those who moved in more affluent circles were not immune to the increasing feeling that the Gospel needed to be applied in the real non-clerical world of poverty and exploitation. A group of middle-class evangelical Christians, later known as the Clapham Saints, who included bankers, politicians and East India Company civil servants, more or less invented pressure group politics by their persistant campaigning against slavery. Leading the campaign was a small wiry man called William Wilberforce who had no intention of letting his fellow Christians rest easy. John Briggs says that Wilberforce's book *The Practical View*, contrasted the life of what he called the real Christian and the life of the merely nominal Christian. For him, nominal Christianity was worse than useless: if you believe, then your behaviour should correspond, in his view, and this what he had said from the 1780s onwards. He followed the pioneering work done by the Quakers for the abolitionist cause and one of the most striking things about all these reformers is their sheer patience. It took Wilberforce twenty years to achieve the abolition of the slave trade in 1807, and another quarter of a century before emancipation was gained – nearly half a century of work. These men had to be the sort of people who would really stay with an issue once they had taken it up; they needed that immense patience. Before they could get a parliamentary vote they had to create public opinion. They had to become masters of propaganda. For example, they persuaded Wedgwood to produce his famous little cameo of a slave with his hands raised kneeling in prayers, and the legend, 'Am I not a slave and also a brother?' – the brotherhood of man was part of the thinking behind the abolitionist cause.

This growing tendency to see Christianity as an international faith led many Victorians to the mission field. Roman Catholic missionary activity was long established, but the early nineteenth century brought the reformed traditions fully into the missionary fray with a host of missionary organisations being founded.

Victorian missionaries are now much criticised for their paternalism – a charge which is not always justified. They included in their number many remarkable self-sacrificing men and women, like the former cobbler's apprentice turned Baptist minister, William Carey. Michael Smith, church historian and minister at Golcar in Yorkshire, tells of the ministers' meeting where Carey suggested, simply on the basis of his reading of the New Testament, that some thought ought to be given to their obligations to the heathen overseas. One particularly crusty old minister by the name of Riley said to him, 'Sit down, young man; if the Lord wants to convert the heathen he'll do it in his own way without us doing anything.'

Carey was not, however, to be put down so easily, and he continued his investigations into the matter and finally produced a small book with the rather splendid title *An Enquiry into the Obligations of Christians as to the Means to the Conversion of the Heathen in which the Religious Faith of the Different Nations of the World, the Success of Former Undertakings and the Practicability of Further Undertakings are Considered*, published in Leicester, where he had gone to be a minister, in 1792. In the same year he gathered together twelve ministers and a ministerial student at a meeting at the home of Mrs Wallis, a widow in Kettering, and together they founded the Baptists' Missionary Society on the basis of a collection which amounted to the considerable sum (for those days) of thirteen pounds, two shillings and sixpence.

As missionary activity overseas became more acceptable, and the campaign against slavery gained momentum, a new criticism began to be levelled at Christians intent on reform and mission. As John Briggs says, one way of getting at the early Evangelicals was to say that they were only interested in black slaves overseas and not in white slaves in the factories in Yorkshire and Lancashire. It is a slander on them because although some of them certainly specialised in the abolitionist campaign, others specialised just as much in the problems of the industrial North, and as time went on more and more of them awoke to the abuses that were going on in Britain's mills and factories. The big name here is that of the Earl of Shaftesbury. Admittedly, he came into the movement initially not so much as as pro-worker as what you might call an anti-mill-owner. He was an aristocrat who did not like the new money, and one way of getting at it was to attack the conditions of labour in the factories which produced it. But as he became acquainted with city conditions his sympathies were won over for the workers themselves, and he became deeply in-

Those fighting for the abolition of slavery under the leadership of William Wilberforce became masters of publicity. This cameo produced by Wedgwood was part of their dogged campaign

volved in the campaign for reforming the factories, particularly with regard to working hours and the regulation of dangerous machinery. This was only part of his work. For almost sixty years this remarkable man was chairman of the Metropolitan Lunacy Commission and its national successor. Shaftesbury was an exceptional man. Many people within the Establishment, and particularly the religious Establishment, were opposed both to social and to parliamentary reform. John Briggs points out that one difficulty for the Church of England in particular was the way the bishops had voted on the Reform Bill – mostly, against, which was why the Church was in such danger in 1832. There is an informative little rhyme that was supposed to have been recited on Guy Fawkes' Night in 1832:

Remember, remember that God is the sender
Of every good gift unto man;
But the devil to spite us sent fellows in mitres
To rob us of all that they can.

This was the time when the Bishop of Bristol's palace was burnt down – the Church had a very bad image because of its attitude to reform. Shaftesbury and his friends were not, of course, political radicals; they were Tories. But they were compassionate Tories, much concerned with the real conditions that stared them in the eye – huge urban problems that the State was simply not dealing with. Shaftesbury had one encounter with a boy who had spent the previous winter living in the inside of a huge lawn-roller in Regent's Park. It was that kind of situation which made them realise they had to do something to improve the awful living conditions of the slum dwellers and the ragged children on the streets of London. Tackling things like this with the Ragged Schools led them to the further problems of shelter for the Ragged School pupils, and then the task of finding employment for them, which in turn led to the Shoeblacks' Brigades.

There was more than enough to occupy Shaftesbury and his friends at home. But this increasing social commitment was accompanied by the feeling that it was the duty of Christians in Europe to share the benefits of medicine and education as well as of faith with countries outside Europe.

The young David Livingstone, no stranger himself to deprivation, was one of those to be inspired by that ideal. Dr Brian Stanley, Tutor in

Church History at Trinity College, Bristol, describes how Livingstone grew up in a one-room home in a tenement owned by the local cotton mill in Blantyre. He started work at the age of ten as a 'piecer' – tying together cotton fibres which were in danger of breaking. He worked Monday to Saturday from six in the morning until eight at night and then went on to the company's night school until ten, when he went home and did some extra reading. His parents were orthodox Calvinists who originally belonged to the Church of Scotland and later joined the Independent or Congregational Church. They taught him the essentials of the Christian faith, but he himself testified to the fact that in his late teens he made that faith a matter of personal commitment and determined to devote his life to the alleviation of human suffering.

Livingstone was not a natural student but, convinced of his missionary vocation, he struggled his way through medical and theological studies. He then turned his attention to South Africa. Brian Stanley says that his concern was to press northwards beyond the frontiers of European influence, where he believed that the Africans would respond more readily to the Christian message. So he moved into what is now Botswana, but he only made one conversion – a Botswana chief, who later lapsed somewhat because he wanted to keep more than one wife. Livingstone then moved further north, right up to the Zambezi River, because he had a tremendous vision of it as a highway for bringing Christianity and commerce into Central Africa. That was where he spent the later stages of his life. He made his remarkable trans-African journey between 1854 and 1856, and the aim of which was, precisely, to establish whether the Zambezi could fulfil a missionary function, with a special object of stamping out the slave trade.

He saw himself as the friend of the Africans, but he did also believe that the only remedy for the ills of Africa (which in fact were very largely caused by the white man) was Christianity plus economic regeneration by God-fearing traders from Great Britain – and of course he has been much criticised for that.

Livingstone does not confirm to the image of a narrow-minded religious imperialist. He was as much an explorer as a missionary – although he was an explorer with a Christian motive. In the same way William Carey was not only a missionary but also a practical interpreter of Indian culture. Michael Smith emphasises what an outstanding linguist Carey was. Many of the versions of the Scriptures in the languages of

India were first made by Carey, and it is also significant that the two chief helpers who came out to him, a schoolmaster and a printer, worked with him not only on these translations of the Scriptures but on Carey's translation and editing of the great Hindu classic, the *Ramayana* – the idea being that this would help people coming out to India to understand Indian culture so that the Gospel could be preached in a way that Indians would find understandable and acceptable. He founded with his friends a kind of independent Indian Church in which Indian converts were treated as full members right from the start.

For all the undoubted gifts of individual Victorian missionaries it is undeniable that they have gained a reputation for cultural high-handedness and interference. A fair charge? Dr Peter Cotterell, Principal of the London Bible College and himself a missionary for twenty years in Ethiopia, admits that many of the nineteenth-century missionaries did feel that the people of Africa and India were poor and deprived and sometimes they used the word 'ignorant' too readily. However there were practices in these countries which offended the conscience of the missionaries. For example, in parts of Nigeria in the nineteenth century identical twins were considered definitely bad news and were buried alive at birth. In parts of India a widow was expected to burn herself to death on her husband's funeral pyre, and the missionaries undoubtedly tried to interfere with that practice; even the missionaries in this century have encountered the practice, in Arabia, of trying to burn out the devils which were considered to be the cause of dysentery by placing a red hot coal on a baby's stomach, and they had no qualms about intervening. So when missionaries are criticised for meddling with indigenous cultures it is only fair to insist on specific instances if a judgement is to be made about right or wrong. However, it can certainly be accepted that nineteenth-century Englishmen did interfere with culture. Christianity does interfere with culture, British or American or any other culture as well as Indian or African. This can hardly be avoided, because culture is the sum of everything that we do and Christianity has got something to say about everything we do.

Of course, Christianity is itself influenced. The short-term effects of the French Revolution were obvious. It was also to have more sinister long-term results. Dom Aidan Bellenger's judgement is that the net gainers from the Revolution in many ways were the Jews and the Protestants, who were given a much wider role in French society and accepted into it, whereas before the Revolution you had to be a Catholic to be properly part of French society, with a Catholic wedding and baptism being the nearest there was to civil registration.

But this gain was a mixed blessing, because as the mythology of counter-revolutionary historiography developed, the very fact that these concessions had been made to the Jews and the Protestants gave rise to the idea that these people were at the centre of a plot to undermine the State. The idea that the Revolution was created by groups of Enlightenment-orientated Protestants, Jews and Freemasons is a myth that emerges from the very start among the writers who opposed the Revolution, most of them clerics. So although Protestants and Jews gained in the short run, in the longer perspective it was not an entirely satisfactory outcome for them; for example, some of the gross anti-Semitism which developed at the end of the nineteenth century had its origins in the emigration of these clergy to England and elsewhere.

Predicting the results of human endeavour has never been easy. Livingstone went to Africa as a missionary and by doing so affected more than that continent's religious beliefs. Brian Stanley thinks that as a missionary in many ways Livingstone could be judged a failure because he only ever made one convert whose conversion was short lived; but his real achievement was the opening up of Africa to missionary work. After his death there was a thrust into Central Africa on several fronts at once; the Church of Scotland and the Free Church went into Malawi, the Church Missionary Society went into Uganda as a direct result of an appeal by Stanley shortly after Livingstone's death, the London Missionary Society went into the Lake Tanganyika area and the Baptists, after Stanley had travelled the length of the Congo River, came into the Congo Basin from the west.

The whole explosion of missionary work into Central Africa in the late 1870s is in many ways a direct consequence of Livingstone's work. But so of course was the entry of the European imperial powers; without Livingstone the scramble for Africa which took place in the mid 1880s would not have taken place in the way that it did. Whatever your view, it has to be said that Livingstone shaped the course of Africa in the late nineteenth century more than anyone else.

Livingstone's achievement was not an unmixed blessing, in the same way that the French Revolution had not been an unmitigated curse for the Church it attacked. Dom Aidan Bellenger thinks that for the

Church the pluses and the minuses did not always work out in the way you might have expected. One very big positive result was in the foundation of new religious orders for women; some of them were explicit attempts to atone for the Revolution, but others were a reflection of a change in attitudes towards women, endorsing a more active life for them. Some of these orders, notably the Sisters of Charity, had their main impact in France, but they had a powerful effect throughout Europe and in England too: a great many primary schools and hospitals and so on owe their origins to these French religious orders. All this was of course part of a wider movement in which the Church started to look beyond Europe to a wider world; French nineteenth-century colonialism had its ecclesiastical parallel in the movement of French clergy, French religious and French laypeople trying to evangelise Africa.

Revolution, reform and revival also had an effect on the religious possibilities opening up for women in England. Olive Anderson, Professor of History at Queen Mary and Westfield College, London, thinks that the Evangelical Revival had a significant impact on the religious activities of women. It is sometimes even said that the Revival feminised religion, but it is probably more accurate to say that in terms of the Revival the perfect born-again Christian was conceived as a submissive, pure, obedient person who was very much not of this world – and that at the time those were precisely the sort of qualities that were associated with women and admired in them; the born-again Christian was after all very much someone who made the home and the church or chapel the centre of activity. The more you think of Christianity in this way, the larger the part women and family life will play, and there is indeed what has sometimes been called a maternal domestic culture which goes hand in hand with the Evangelical Revival. Certainly that revival had passed its peak by the early Victorian period, but it remains one of the main sources of a particular way of thinking about the role of women in church activity which had become a very powerful imperative by the middle of the nineteenth century; so much so that there were very few women indeed who did not, either consciously or unconsciously, respond to it.

CHAPTER VII

MONKEYS, MYSTERY AND MODERNISM

'The view which most naturalists until recently entertained – that each species has been independently created – is erroneous.'

Charles Darwin, one time theological student setting the evolutionary cat among the creationist pigeons.

'Is it through your grandfather or your grandmother that you claim descent from an ape?'

Bishop Wilberforce of Oxford, Soapy Sam as he was known, cross-examining Darwin's friend and supporter T. H. Huxley at a meeting of the British Association in Oxford in 1860.

Contrary to popular belief, the Victorian age was no calm religious backwater of uneventful and docile piety. The Christian churches found themselves under attack. So far we have spoken about reform of church structures, usually brought about by those within the churches. In these years the churches, all the churches, do not set the pace of reforming thought. They respond with varying degrees of success to the vast changes all around them. The move from a rural to an industrial economy, the pressure of mechanical work, advances in science and palaeontology, and the power of newspapers all come into play.

The questions and controversies which buffet the Christian churches today have their roots in an agenda set more than a century ago. These are the years which gave birth to the great trinity of 'isms' – Marxism, agnosticism and modernism – which still harry and challenge the churches. Most important of all, this was the time when the undebatable was thrown open to discussion. Who or what was Man? Was he the loved child of a creator God or the chance product of a natural process?

The literalist game was certainly up but there was much more to protest about and to explore. The work of the old reformers had now to be reformed. As well as crushing social deprivation there was a hunger for mystery and faith. In this chapter we follow the unforeseen consequences of the clerical old boy network, meet a blue-stocking who objected to Sunday hairdressing and follow the career of a pawnbroker turned general and of one illustrious – or notorious – convert. There is some siege mentality but also some prophetic vision.

But first let us begin at the beginning – right at the beginning. In 1830 Sir Charles Lyell in his *Principles of Geology* argued convincingly that the world was much older than commonly believed. By counting backwards, the ingenious sixteenth-century Church of Ireland divine, James Ussher, had worked out that the world was created in 4004 BC. This was now revealed to be nonsense. The Bible was not to be relied upon as a scientific handbook. Worse was to follow from the pen of Charles Darwin.

The Darwins were freethinkers but young Charles's upbringing had been far from irreligious. Dr James Moore, lecturer in History of Science at the Open University, thinks that it is very important to understand that Darwin came from a Unitarian background on his mother's side, the Wedgwoods. The Darwins were rather more freethinking than that – perhaps not even Christians at all – but Charles went with his mother to the Unitarian chapel in the High Street at Shrewsbury, and to the school run by its minister, Mr Case. Early nineteenth-century Unitarians believed in the Bible very much as conservative Christians do today, but they believed in it so strictly that they refused to accept the doctrine of the Trinity, because they could not find it taught anywhere in the Bible. They attached great significance to biblical miracles and in particular of course to the resurrection as the promise of future life. They also tended to be rationalists in religious matters, elevating human reason above religious feeling, and they produced great scholars, like the distinguished scientist, chemist and theologian Joseph Priestley. This was the kind of influence under which Darwin grew up.

Charles Darwin was sent to Edinburgh University to read medicine. It was not a successful move. Charles loathed the anatomy theatre and hated medical lectures. His interests lay more towards the natural sciences. Dr Darwin, his father, gave up any hopes for a medical career for Charles and directed his son to Cambridge and to theology with a view to ordination in the Anglican Church and to an undistinguished but pleasant life as a country parson.

That was the sort of pragmatic attitude towards Anglican orders which was being increasingly questioned by a pressure group for reform within the Church of England led by a nineteenth-century gang of four, Pusey, Keble, Manning and Newman. The movement was known as the Oxford or Tractarian Movement. Geoffrey Rowell, Chaplain, Fellow and Tutor at Keble College, Oxford, says the university cities were places of much more ecclesiastical significance than they are today. Oxford and Cambridge in particular produced the young clergy who were going to serve the Church and influence it. What you can see in the Oxford Movement is the beginning of a much increased professional concern about the clergy, because out of it (though not only out of it alone) came the founding of the theological colleges.

The Oxford Movement drew into itself a great religious impetus derived from a variety of sources. It shared with the Evangelicals a concern for active holiness, the challenge to the Church really to live the Gospel, and it drew from the Romantic movement the sense of wonder and mystery in reaction against the attitudes of the Enlightenment. It rediscovered imagination, symbolism and sacrament, and it rediscovered the Fathers of the Church and the Catholic continuity of the Church of England – because the question of Anglican identity was a sharp one. Its message was, do not trust to your political privileges; trust to your apostolic commission and its continuity from the earliest days of the Church. In this way the Church of England, which had indisputable Reformation influences and had become very accustomed to thinking of itself as a Protestant Church, found itself challenged about its Catholic roots and Catholic continuity.

Charles Darwin had a more relaxed attitude towards his theology. Thanks to the clerical old boy network, he secured a place on the vessel HMS Beagle as a self-financing gentleman companion to the aristocratic evangelical captain Robert Fitzroy. The ship was bound for the south Americas on a surveying expedition. The adventure was to change Darwin's life and not least his understanding of creation. He was astonished by what he saw. James Moore quotes his saying that his mind was a 'chaos of delight'. When he walked into a tropical forest for the first time in Brazil he jotted down notes to himself – 'tresses entwining tresses',

'glorious creepers, beautiful butterflies, halleluja!' It was for him a religious experience. He reacted to nature in a romantic way, as he experienced the rainforest or an earthquake or the first sight of the naked
Fuegian savages at the very southernmost tip of South America. But none
of this prevented him from wanting to explain what he saw.

At this period he had conventional views about the creation: God had
designed the world and brought it into existence rapidly, miraculously – a
long time ago, for he did accept modern geology and was no literalist
believer in the Book of Genesis. He did think it was appropriate to
understand in terms of God's laws not only the heavens, *à la* Newton, but
the earth as well, and not only the crust of the earth but the origination of
plant life, animal life and human life as well. Gradually during the long
voyage he framed a set of questions which he was to spend the rest of his
life answering. He did not have the answers by the end of the voyage but
he did have an agenda.

When he returned to England, Charles did not rush into print. He
knew evolution, or the transmutation of species, was controversial and he
had no wish to be tarred with an anti-establishment brush. He settled
down to a quiet life, not in Anglican orders, but to all intents and
purposes living in the style of a country parson.

Away from the evolutionist arena, others were less cautious about
rocking the establishment boat – among them a remarkable woman called
Hannah More. Hannah had been jilted four times by the same man.
Overcome by guilt, he provided her with private means. She moved from
her home in south-west England to London where she mixed in blue
stocking and literary circles and gained a reputation as a dramatist. Later
in life she became involved with the evangelical Clapham Sect and at the
bidding of William Wilberforce, the anti-slavery campaigner, turned her
back on literary London and concentrated on the problem of the rural
poor. Fran Beckett of the Shaftesbury Society thinks it would be fair to
describe her as a controversial figure, and also a very influential one. She
wrote prolifically – religious tracts and pamphlets and more substantial
works as well, all geared towards looking at the effects of religion on
everyday life. Her work was quite moralistic in tone – often little homilies
or sermons, almost nineteenth-century parables. They were written in a
language very accessible to ordinary people, trying to help them think
about simple Christian values. They were immensely popular. One pamphlet ran into over two million copies. She had her hobby horses as well.

Charles Darwin, the one-time theological student who reacted to nature in a romantic way but also wanted to explain what he saw

Hannah More, the much-jilted and much-read pamphleteer,
who had strong views about hair dressing on Sunday
and pioneered education for the rural poor

She was very indignant about hairdressers coming on Sundays to do gentlewomen's hair – she felt that Sunday should be properly observed as a day of worship and rest, not as an opportunity for wealthy women to abuse poorer female labour. Some of her views earned her some antagonism. She wrote in a way which was, for her day, quite feminist – for example, she was very critical of men who viewed women simply as adornments for social gatherings, and was just as critical of women who she felt colluded with them in this.

Hannah believed it was just as important to recognise the educational and religious needs of the rural poor as it was to be aware of their city counterparts. The balance between town and country was shifting dramatically and for the first time in the history of religious protest and reform there are the statistics to prove it. In 1851 a nationwide census of church attendance was held. John Briggs explains that it all began partly because people were worried that there were not enough churches in urban areas. The initial enquiry was about the number of church seats available, but the question was also asked about how many people went to church. It was found that they were about one and a half million church seats short in urban areas. What finally came out of the enquiry was that of those available to go to church on the particular Sunday chosen for the survey, 50 per cent did not go. Today this would be considered as quite a vote of confidence in the Church, but at the time the Church of England felt obliged to come up with excuses.

As Horace Mann, the Government spokesman, said, you could not presume that because 50 per cent were absent that Sunday they would be absent every Sunday, and it was pointed out that the previous Sunday had been Mothering Sunday and it was a bit unreasonable to expect everyone to go to church for two Sundays in a row. Also, there seems to have been storms which affected Anglican churches but not Nonconfirmist ones – preferential weather, as it were. Of the churchgoers, about 50 per cent went to Anglican churches and about 50 per cent to Nonconformist chapels and Roman Catholic churches, though the Roman Catholic numbers were very small. The one thing which really struck people was that church attendance was lowest in the new industrial towns and cities in the industrial Midlands and North, and this was what worried them.

In Nottingham a young pawnbroker became a Christian. Convinced of the need to bring the Gospels to the poor, he began preaching in the streets. He moved down to London and gave up pawnbroking for full-time ministry. His name was William Booth. He was ordained as a Methodist minister in 1858 but his unorthodox methods quickly provoked criticism. He eventually set up a 'Christian mission' in a tent in Whitechapel. That mission would turn into a worldwide army. General Eva Burroughs, leader of the Salvation Army, says the mission gradually grew and the missioners developed their dynamic compulsion to go out and preach their message. For the working class of this period, with their long, hard working hours and few enjoyments, the mission meetings were exciting. The Salvation Army became an army in a rather curious way – neither a deliberate plan on the part of William Booth nor something that happened by pure chance. The movement simply began to feel it was on the march against sin, evil, oppression, poverty and injustice, and its members began to say, 'We are the army of God and this is our captain.'

Eventually a pamphlet was produced which used the phrase 'We are a volunteer army', and William Booth struck out the word 'volunteer' and said, 'No, we are a Salvation Army'. As if by some kind of inspiration the members of the movement began to say that they wanted him as their General, not General Secretary, and the ordained clergy in the movement became known as officers, and so the terminology of the Army of God developed.

The Salvationists were inspired of course by Scripture, with its references to being soldiers of Jesus Christ and putting on the whole armour of God to go out and fight against evil – such concepts of these, and great hymns like 'Onward Christian Soldiers', were part of a structure which was not invented by the Salvation Army. To this day the Salvation Army speaks of itself as an army mobilised by God and works very much by command; there is not much sitting about and arguing in committees.

William Booth, now General Booth, had no qualms about using lively exuberant music to attract people to his meetings. Others were not so sure. John Briggs quotes Lord Shaftesbury describing the Army as a trick of the devil who, have failed to make Christianity odious, was now trying to make it ridiculous. But Booth was undoubtedly on the right lines in getting on to the cultural wavelength of the working class, as with his famous question, 'Why should the devil have all the best tunes?'. He believed that the situation was so serious that if you were going to go into

General William Booth, the founder of the Salvation Army who decided that the devil should not have all the best tunes and that women should not be debarred from positions of authority

the slums and do anything effective you really did need something like military discipline.

William Booth and his army were not the only people trying to wake up the established church. In their own very different way, leaders of the Oxford Movement were trying to achieve the same end. Fr Geoffrey Rowell emphasises that the Oxford Movement certainly wanted to reform the Church. They thought that there were many clergy who were idle and certainly not committed to any high ideal of holiness of life and did not really teach their parishioners. They were, of course, already the heirs of movements such as that which founded the Sunday Schools. The importance of education is obvious and it has to be remembered that for a time the Church tried to educate the whole nation. In the end that proved to be beyond its capacity, but if you look around country parishes today you can still see standing, even if sold off, not only the vicarages and rectories but the Victorian parochial schools. A good many of these arose out of the Oxford Movement.

There were those who were suspicious of the Oxford Movement and accused its leaders of trying to reverse the Reformation. Reformers of any description had to tread warily. Even Hannah More, loyal to the Church of England all her life, was attacked for her Sunday Schools. The initial ideal, says Fran Beckett, was to have Sunday Schools that would teach poor children about the Bible, but very quickly it was realised that it was necessary to teach them in a wider sense – how to read, how to write, and how to manage money. As they got older, they needed help to prepare them for housekeeping and other work.

The Bible education rapidly broadened out. The problem was that the local landed gentry and affluent farmers did not take to it very kindly. They saw education of poor people as subversive. Hannah More had one particularly bad period when she came under very heavy criticism for the way in which the children in her schools were being taught. The criticism came from the Church of England itself and at the heart of it was an accusation of what was for the Church of England the heresy of all heresies – Methodism. And this was largely because the prayers used at Hannah's school were extempory and therefore suspect.

To add insult to injury, the Methodists then weighed in and accused Hannah of poaching people from Methodist chapels. Hannah was bitterly hurt. She had been a pioneer but as the century grew older it became more usual for women and not only middle-class women to become active Christians rather than merely passive churchgoers. Olive Anderson, Professor of History at London University, says that vast numbers of middle-class women embarked upon social work, including the care of the suffering and the care for physical and material well-being of the poor. Working-class women as well as the leisured middle-class became involved. This came about particularly through the development of the so-called Bible Women whom Mrs Ranyard began to organise in the 1860s. These were working-class women who were paid, and who, it is true, worked under the supervision of a 'lady', but were given an enormous amount of discretion and initiative. They went round the neediest areas in the big cities bringing the Gospel to the poor and also nursing, helping, advising and being quite prepared to get down to the basics of cooking and cleaning and the rest of the household chores. The idea was that you could only really get to women living on the margin of society through asking women, who were like them, to go and work with them.

Increasingly those involved in working with the poor came to realise that it was not enough to preach to people. It was this realisation, not Victorian prudery, that inspired the many church-led crusades against alcohol. John Briggs thinks that in many respects you can rightly call Victorian society a drink-sodden society, and it is important to realise that in the nineteenth century the temperance crusade was not just a matter of prissy individual conscience-hawking, the concern was as much for the drunkard's family as for the drunkard himself. We may laugh now at Victorian songs with titles like 'Sell No More Drink to my Father', but it was no joke – Father plus drink could literally be a terror. The drink issue had a huge social dimension. As with the slavery issue earlier in the century, there was a strong awareness that you needed a positive cultural factor at work as well as a negative one of legislative control. You could control drink by legislation up to a point, by such things as limiting drinking hours, but you could not control it very much. More important was what you might call the alternative culture: for instance the Temperance Excursions (Thomas Cook comes on the scene here) on the railways and billiard halls, which were initially temperance-inspired. This was also perhaps one of the reasons why churches in the second half of the nineteenth century became increasingly institutional. Chapel became something all-embracing, not just for Sundays; on every day of the week there would be something going on – drama groups, rambling clubs, cycling clubs. Mutual improvement societies, 'dry' friendly societies to offset the boozy ones that met in the pubs. It was what you might call a total cultural package.

Members of the Oxford Movement were also much involved in working among the poorest of city dwellers. In spite of its name the Oxford Movement was not an ivory tower exercise. In its earliest days it gained its other name 'The Tractarian Movement' from the pamphlets it distributed all over the country. The Tractarian dispute was a nationwide crusade, not a private academic argument. In today's language it was more like the anti-poll tax campaign than a series of Reith lectures – and the advent of national newspapers meant that the literate middle-classes could make up their own minds about the various types of churchmanship on offer.

Loyalties were not immutable. Of the original gang of four, Keble and Pusey stayed in the Anglican church and Manning and Newman took the path to Rome. Manning became cardinal and Archbishop of Westminster. Newman, an even greater catch for the Roman Catholic Church, was given a rougher ride. After studying for the priesthood, he was ordained and worked quietly in Birmingham. He then accepted an invitation to become rector of the new Catholic University in Dublin. Newman was an enthusiastic convert but also a realistic one. Roman Catholic or Anglican, he was still a protester at heart. Fr Ian Kerr, a Catholic priest and former Chaplain at Oxford, explains that Newman had already seen something of the limitations of the Roman Catholic Church while in Rome – he realised, for example, that things were at a low ebb theologically. But it was his Dublin experience which really showed him how the Church worked in practice. He discovered that the laity were ignored and neglected, and he experienced the high-handed ways in which the bishops behaved. In Dublin he had been particularly concerned with the neglect of the laity because he wanted to try to get them to contribute money to the university, and you could not get them to contribute if they were to have no hand in the running of it. When he returned to England in 1859 he soon became involved in a controversy about the rights of the English Catholic laity in education, and that was what led him to writing his first theological essay as a Catholic, *On Consulting the Faithful on Matters of Doctrine*.

As the years wore on he became more involved in controversy because the Catholic Church was becoming increasingly ultramontane, that is to say, there was a movement pressing for the definition of papal infallibility and emphasising papal supremacy and the centralisation of Roman Catholic Church affairs. Newman became more and more involved in these debates, and gradually over the years began to hammer out a theology of the Church and of the limits and meaning of papal infallibility. The upshot was that Newman became a highly controversial figure in the Roman Catholic Church; he met with considerable opposition and hostility and was under a cloud for a long time.

In many ways Newman was before his time as a Roman Catholic. His views of the limitations of papal infallibility were not shared by the long-lived Pio Nono, Pius IX, who in 1869 called the First Vatican Council to confront the problem of how his Church should deal with the modern world. How was an emphasis on papal infallibility supposed to answer that problem? Dom Aidan Bellenger explains that when the actual doctrine of papal infallibility was defined in 1870 there was considerable opposition to it among the bishops of the Roman Catholic Church, but the great majority were none the less in favour of it, because in their view infallibility answered the need for some kind of spiritual authority in the face of all the undermining doctrines of nineteenth-century theological and political life. Liberalism, freethinking, and a whole range of views associated with Romanticism particularly were attacked by the Pope in his *Syllabus of Errors* of 1864, and the view of the authority of his Church which he put forward was one in which that Church stood alone as an institution which could put forward the truth in a world where there were now many truths. His view of infallibility was that the Pope spoke for the Christian Church and spoke with great authority in a world where all previous authority seemed under challenge.

That stress on papal infallibility helped to define the Oxford Movement which was proud to draw on a Catholic heritage but unwilling to accept papal authority. Today the Anglo-Catholic wing of the Church of England is regarded as the direct heir of the Movement. But in reality the legacy is much more widely spread. Fr Geoffrey Rowell says that the Oxford Movement undoubtedly enriched the Church of England by recovering so much from the past. Even churches which would today be regarded as rather Low Church can have architecture influenced by the Oxford Movement, and things which were regarded as popish – colour, banners, even flowers – returned as a result of the influences of the movement and the subsequent 'Catholic Revival'. This still continues within the Church of England today in sacramental practice and in the place of the Eucharist as the central act of worship for many parish churches.

The Oxford Movement also opened up opportunities for women in the Church of England by starting up convents and monasteries for contemplative and active nuns, but it has to be said that the Salvation Army far outstripped all the other nineteenth-century reform movements in the sexual equality stakes. General Eva Burroughs says that when referring to the Salvation Army inside the Army, you talk not only about 'our Founder', William Booth, but about 'our Founders', because his wife Catherine played a very significant part in the Army's early growth and development. She was an extremely intellectual woman, well read and well versed in the Scriptures, and she felt that the Scriptures made it quite clear that women have gifts that must be used in the service of God. She took seriously the words of St Paul, 'neither male nor female', and felt that women had a special role in being able to preach the message of Jesus with particular sensitivity and concern for the individual, and in all this she greatly influenced her husband's thinking.

When women were given that opportunity, over a hundred years ago, they seized upon it, and in the Salvation Army they have had two great privileges: to be ordained to the ministry and preach, and to have any position equal with men in the movement. From the very beginning a woman might be the Salvation Army equivalent of a bishop, and often a woman would be in charge of a mission with a man as her assistant – which was quite revolutionary over a hundred years ago.

And that would still be revolutionary nowadays in the vast majority of Christian churches. Not all reform stands the passage of time. Using hindsight could the First Vatican Council in 1869 really be said to be a reform? Was it not a backward step? Dom Aidan Bellenger thinks that on balance it was not. He says that looked at from the perspective of the end of the present century, the First Vatican Council allowed the Roman Catholic Church to survive into this century because it concentrated on the spiritual as opposed to the political. It concentrated perhaps too much on the centralisation of the Church in Rome and in the person of the Pope but this gave the papacy an international authority beyond politics which otherwise it would have lacked. Of course it carried the danger of bureaucratic centralisation and the narrowness that goes with it. Looked at in a wider context, however, it can be argued that it was a means of projecting the Roman Catholic Church into the twentieth century and making sure that the papacy was not just some antique remnant of Renaissance Italy.

The papacy was no longer an Italian principality. After Pius IX died, Leo XIII, a more liberal Pope, made John Henry Newman a cardinal. Looking ahead many say the First Vatican Council then was the necessary precursor to the Second Vatican Council of 1962 and many also say that Newman, the former Anglican, was the true architect of that great twentieth-century reforming council. Fr Ian Kerr says that having become a Roman Catholic Newman went on in his own time to become a liberal Roman Catholic, and you can take the view that his theological significance for the Roman Catholic Church today lies first of all in the ways in which he anticipated the Second Vatican Council. His whole teaching on the Church was in very close accord with what the Second Vatican Council taught. But in addition to this he was very important because of his position at what might be called the extreme centre – in many ways a liberal Catholic but also a very loyal and traditional one, holding together, as you might say, the Left and the Right. He was declared Venerable by the Pope in January 1992, and that is the first step towards canonisation, and if he is canonised, as seems likely, he is also likely to be declared a Doctor of the Church. For Roman Catholics that means something much more than a particularly able, high-powered and prolific theologian; it means someone whom the Church is designating specifically as a teacher of Christians, and it may well be that Newman will come to be seen as the Doctor *par excellence* of the period in which we are living, as St Thomas Aquinas is accepted by the Roman Catholic Church as the Doctor of the Middle Ages.

And what about Mr Darwin and those monkeys? Darwin delayed publication of his theory for as long as he could. Finally, when faced with the prospect of being pipped at the post by someone else, he hurried into print. He knew he was raising more than a convincing scientific argument, he was voicing questions which would occupy the churches for generations to come. Dr James Moore quotes from Darwin's private notebooks in which he writes 'It falls, the fabric falls', and when he says 'fabric' he does not just mean the social fabric; he means the whole order of things sanctioned by Anglican religion. Everything changes once you accept that people might evolve from molluscs. That is not of course to say that it becomes an irreligious order of things; but it does become ultimately for Darwin a non-Christian order of things. For Huxley and the Young Turks of the 1860s it becomes in fact a new religious order in which scientists, not clergymen, are the priests; naturalists, geologists, biologists and psychologists interpret Nature for us, not ecclesiastics.

Darwin himself gave up Christianity, but this does not have to be attributed necessarily to his theory, because it was possible to accept it and remain a Christian, as many examples from the late nineteenth century show. Darwin did not in fact create a conflict between science and religion; he raised up new questions which had existed perennially among the churches and within science as it had been practised in his time by Christian gentlemen amateurs. Questions of the evil in the world, of the purpose of things which did not seem to have any purpose – these were the kind of questions he asked afresh and made them acute and undeniable. Lots of people had been evolutionists before him – in fact, it was an increasingly respectable view during his lifetime – but the really difficult aspect of the doctrine was the notion that human beings, body and soul, in their totality, had come from animals.

This was not just an aesthetic problem but an acute moral problem; and after Darwin it would not go away.

CHAPTER VIII

A WORLD SHAKEN BY WAR

The first half of the twentieth century carries an unwieldy burden of death, revolution, horror and war. At many times and for many people paradise was far away and hell an all too present reality. Christians were caught in a trap between heroism and survival. A few chose the hard path. The story of Christian protest from the late 1800s to 1950 is dominated by an absence of protest, by the shameful silence of those who knew the truth about the concentration camps but shut their eyes against what they did not want to see and, to protect themselves and their families, pretended that sanity ruled in the mad house.

But before the perversion of humanity that was Hitler dominated world events, many seeds of protest and renewal had been sown which would only begin to grow after the darkness of Nazism receded. The years before the Second World War were years of prophecy which are only beginning to be fulfilled in our time. As technology advanced ever more quickly, throughout its various traditions, Christianity threw down a challenge of simplicity; as the world became more and more bitterly divided, some Christians began to dream about a form of reconciliation which would be a way of affirming, not betraying, their faith.

In pursuit of the story of religious protest in the first half of this century we shall meet heroes and villains. We shall come across cosiness, courage, vision and common sense. We shall encounter an over-moneyed wastrel, a spinner of fairytales, a wise grandmother and arguably the most successful mass evangelist known in the history of the Church. Many of those we talk about will have lived by the violence of the times. All will have been touched by it.

This will be no story of triumphalism. Let us begin with an out and out failure – Charles de Foucauld, an aristocratic French playboy who inherited his family fortune at a young age. He decided on a military career and distinguished himself by his obesity and his willingness to spend money like water. While he was serving as an officer in Algeria, it was discovered that the woman he had been passing off as the Viscountess de Foucauld was his mistress not his wife. The powers-that-were took action. Brother Ian, little brother of Jesus and cleaner at Imperial College, London, makes no bones about the fact that Charles was dismissed from the Army for notorious misconduct. He then decided to occupy himself with the exploration of Morocco, then a forbidden country for Europeans as far as the interior was concerned. So he had to go in disguise, and the disguise he chose was that of a Jewish rabbi, accompanied by a genuine Jewish rabbi. This meant that he had to study both Hebrew and Arabic. He spent eighteen months in Morocco, exploring and making meticulous geographical observations and surveying mountains and rivers partly simply for the interest of it and partly with a view to future French penetration of the area. But the most significant thing about this journey is that through the Jews and Muslims whom he met he gained a sense of the adoration of God, especially through the Muslims' regular programme of prayers throughout the day. He was impressed by the sincerity of this practice, and also by the fact that three or four Muslims who gave him lodging and discovered his true identity never revealed the fact, because he was their guest – even though in some cases this was at the risk of their own lives. The adoration of God and the sense of brotherly hospitality impressed him deeply.

When he returned to France he began to write a book about his explorations. During this time he was living close to a cousin who became a kind of second mother to him. She was a genuine but unobtrusive Christian in her own aristocratic way, and once again he was deeply impressed – particularly by the fact that she and other members of his family never reproached him for his way of life but simply accepted him for what he was. He himself says that it was their silence and gentleness which guided him back towards the faith he had once had in childhood.

Influenced by Muslims, Jews and Christians, Charles began his search for God. The one-time libertine and glutton became an ascetic. He gave away his personal fortune and became a Trappist monk, attracted by the simplicity of the life and its emphasis on manual work. He stayed with the Trappists for seven years but left before taking his final vows. It was a life of austerity but also one of security. Charles felt it was not enough. He

Charles de Foucauld, the one-time libertine and glutton who was moved by the faith of Jews and Muslims to search for a new form of Christian religious life

wanted to share in the uncertainty as well as the hardship of poverty. After spending some time in the Holy Land, Charles became convinced there was a need for a new sort of Christian religious life. He returned to North Africa and set about living the Nazareth life among the Jews and Muslims who had first reminded him of man's need for God.

Charles wanted to return to basics. The reformations and councils of church history held no fascination for him. He wanted to return to the simplicity of the Gospels. He was not alone in such a desire. Across the Atlantic radical Christians began arguing that grace came not only through the sacraments or the Bible but also through the Holy Spirit. The movement known as 'Pentecostalism' was controversial. It claimed that 'speaking in tongues' was not an isolated phenomenon belonging to the Acts of the Apostles but that it was a sign of baptism in the Holy Spirit which belonged as much in the twentieth century as the first.

Others were less sure. Professor James Dunn, formerly Professor of New Testament at Durham University, says that Pentecostalism, when it began in the 1900s in California and the southern states of America, was just regarded as one of the many Christian radical groups that the new world produced; it was not taken seriously until much later. Western European culture has always emphasised and even over-emphasised the rational: unless we can think something through and write it down on paper, we are not going to believe it. Other cultures – the African and Latin-American cultures, for instance – tend to be more integrated, with the rational element not given such an overwhelming priority. You might say that because in Western European culture we are all eggheads to some degree or another and because we curtail other dimensions of the person-ality, many Western intellectuals who enter into charismatic experience claim they have been released and given a fuller experience, a wholeness of Christianity they lacked before.

Many were dubious about the exuberance of the Pentecostalists. Meanwhile the old enthusiasts, the Evangelicals, had lost their reforming zeal and turned their backs on the outside world and went into a holy huddle. Clive Calver, director of the Evangelical Alliance, explains that at the turn of the twentieth century the Evangelicals became obsessed with a form of pre-millenarianism. In other words, they became very much caught up by the idea that Jesus Christ was coming back and would rescue Evangelical Christians out of the world and leave it to stew in its own juice for the next thousand years – which does not exactly give you a strong passion to change things; rather, it gives you a desire to retreat out of your world into some kind of cosy suburban Evangelical ghetto.

That mentality survives today in some of the more extreme fundamentalist groupings, particularly in the United States. But the early years of this century did not lend themselves easily to cosiness. There was an increasing conviction that Christians had concentrated on exclusivity and fragmentation for long enough. Dr Pauline Webb, former Vice Moderator of the Central Committee of the World Council of Churches, says that it all really began with the missionary movement. In the nineteenth century there had been a tremendous expansion of missions right across the world, with all the churches involved. It soon became evident to them that they were almost rivals in the field and this was nonsense. It seems ridiculous to say to someone in Kenya that if you live on one side of the river you belong to the Church of Scotland and if you live on the other side you belong to the Church of England, so it was decided that the churches really must try to work together in a world mission. The International Missionary Conference was convened in 1910 at Edinburgh which was mainly an affair for people from the West – there were very few representatives from the younger nations and younger churches, and of course there were hardly any women.

However, from that conference began a movement towards the unity of the Church, and it also saw the beginning of two other movements. The first was concerned with social justice, and once again it became obvious that separate camps were nonsense and there was a need to pool resources. The second movement was for people who were concerned about the theological differences between the churches and who were hoping to arrive at a theological consensus.

But before long the world had bloodier things to think about than missionary councils. The Great War of 1914–18 began to devour the lives of the young, regardless of theological persuasion. In his desert hermitage Charles de Foucauld, now Brother Charles of Jesus, felt pulled towards Europe and thought of volunteering as a stretcher bearer or chaplain. He stayed in the desert walking towards the death which would claim him before the war ended. He was determined that after the war he would make his new religious order a reality.

Meanwhile the seeds of another revolution in religious life were being sown in the mind of a three-year-old named Roger Schultz, who would become Brother Roger, founder and prior of Taizé. Brother Emil, a member of the Taizé community in France, says Brother Roger tells the story about his grandmother, who, during the First World War, welcomed refugees in the north of France, especially women with babies. At the end of the War she said, 'No-one must ever see again what I have seen, and no-one must ever again go through what I have gone through.' She was one of the last to leave northern Franch on a cattle train as it came under bombardment. One of Brother Roger's earliest memories, when he was three, was seeing his grandmother arrive in Switzerland and hearing her speak these words. She was from a very old Protestant family, and decided she would try to live reconciliation with the Catholic Church through her own life. Her family understood, and no-one thought she was denying her origins.

As the first World War drew to its close, far removed from the horrors of the trenches and the sufferings of the refugees, a young man called Clive Staples Lewis went up to Oxford. C. S. Lewis, who would become famous for his allegorical fairy tales and his combative common-sense approach to Christianity, had turned his back on religion. The dramatist and broadcaster Brian Sibley, says that having chosen the life of an academic, Lewis became famous as a lecturer in English Literature at Oxford but had something else stirring deep down inside him. He often talked about how God had, as he put it, laid traps for him. He used to quote George Herbert's 'Bibles were opened, nets were laid, the world was full of strategems . . .', and in a way, for C. S. Lewis, all his life led towards one particular event – his becoming a Christian in 1931. His whole life changed. He did not leave Oxford, but as a man who had spent all his life thinking about questions of faith and of mystery (mystery was an idea that fascinated him) – mystery in literature and folklore and legend and finally in Christianity – and as a man who grappled with all these things with great effort, he came to a wish to grapple with them on behalf of other people and help other people find their way through what is after all a difficult set of beliefs.

Soon all theological difficulties would be forgotten thanks to a psychopathic Austrian with a remarkable ability to infect others with his sadism. Hitler declared himself the enemy of all Christians. More significantly his manic anti-semitism gave rise to an attempt to wipe out all Jews. Too many churches stayed silent as the concentration camps filled, emptied and filled again. Looking back at the Holocaust who is to blame, the active Nazis or the silent Christians? Rabbi Albert Friedlander,

C. S. Lewis, the spinner of fairy tales and apologist for Christianity who tackled theological questions in plain everyday language

concentration camp survivor and leader of the Westminster Synagogue, thinks that it is very complicated. Christians would like to believe that Hitler was a kind of antichrist and that eventually all the attacks levelled against the Jews were levelled against Christians, but this is not true. Hitler was a psychopath. He hated Jews and in his *Mein Kampf* and his speeches he made it clear he wanted to get rid of every single one of them, and he used them as a kind of scapegoat saying, 'You Germans didn't really lose the War, the Jews lost it for you' – and very popular it all was. Where Christians are concerned, the picture was different. He did recognize that true Christians were his enemies, and so he tried to set up a German Christian Church with the infamous Müller, where Adolf Hitler could be mentioned as part of the liturgy and the churches would know that first obedience always goes to the State. There was the Confessing Church in the 1930s and 1940s, which tried to fight actively against Hitler, with names like Pastor Niemoller and Dietrich Bonhoeffer, around which you can build up the image of a protesting and fighting Church composed of anti-Hitler resisters. But all this still only amounts to a very small group though it did prove that resistance was possible.

Even the Confessing Church with its theology largely formulated by the great Christian teacher, Karl Barth, had its limitations. Its role was primarily defensive. It criticised totalitarianism and the heretical beliefs of the Nazi-organised German Christian Church but it stopped short of outright opposition to Hitler. A few like the theologian Dietrich Bonhoeffer would dare to go the extra mile and put their misgivings into heroic action.

In the early days of the Reich the churches were slow to see what they did not want to see. Bonhoeffer, an academic from an establishment family, was not a rebel by nature, but two days after Hitler came to power he broadcast an attack on the leadership principles of Nazism. The broadcast was cut off mid-air. Bonhoeffer was also the first Christian to attack Hitler's anti-semitism. Rev Edwin Robertson, biographer of Bonhoeffer, recalls that in 1933 Bonhoeffer wrote an article called *The Jewish Question*. Hitler had been making much of those churchmen who were friendly to him, and called themselves 'German Christians', which they certainly were, being much more German than Christian. Bonhoeffer had noticed that Hitler was using Martin Luther and saying that of course Luther had been anti-Semitic, because he was the 'real German Church'. Bonhoeffer quoted Martin Luther's remark, 'If the Jews had treated us

Gentiles in the beginning as we treat the Jews now there would never have been any Gentile Christians', and again his saying, 'We are not yet their equals'. This was not exactly a popular thing to do, to put it mildly.

Bonhoeffer's first concern was the Jews. His second was the Church, for he was desperately worried about the way in which the Church was succumbing, with large sections of both Catholics and Protestants giving in to Hitler. He found himself speaking out against his own Church, and even against those who were actually resisting the inroads of Hitlerian teaching in that Church, because he insisted that it was not enough to say that the Church was being perverted by the German Christians, it was essential to say something also about the Jews. He met with refusal; there was a very brave document declaring church independence – the Barmen Declaration – but Bonhoeffer's paragraph on the Jews was cut out because it was said that it was not timely. So Bonhoeffer more or less gave up as far as the Confessing Church was concerned and came to England in 1934, where he spent two years doing parish work and making friends with George Bell, the Bishop of Chichester. That friendship would be politically significant as well as long-lasting. After his English visit, Bonhoeffer returned to Germany where he quickly became involved in training pastors in an illegal anti-Nazi underground seminary.

His family knew he was in danger and tried to bundle him off to America on a lecture tour. When Bonhoeffer realised the motives behind the tour, he packed his bags and returned to Germany as war was breaking out. Through family connections he became a member of the Abwehr, the German military version of MI5 and there the first conspiracy against Hitler was hatched. This was not an assassination plot. The plan was to arrest Hitler and bring a full list of charges against him.

Bonhoeffer was chosen as the go-between, linking the conspirators and the British government, building on his friendship with Bishop Bell. Edwin Robertson says that in 1942, before the entry of the USA into the war, Bonhoeffer met Bishop Bell and laid the plans before him. He said that if Britain would give a sign that it would deal with a German government that was not a Nazi one, the plan would be put into operation and Germany would discuss a peace treaty. Bishop Bell was very much in favour of this and it appeared that the viability of the idea had been tested by the usual means of wartime intelligence. Anthony Eden was in favour of the plan but Churchill was not, saying, 'When they bring me the head of Adolf Hitler on a charger, then I'll talk to them.' It was

Pastor Dietrich Bonhoeffer, the first Christian to attack Hitler's anti-Semitism and a double agent who was involved in the plot to kill Hitler

probably this which led the plotters to feel that there was only one way out, and that was to assassinate Hitler.

Bonhoeffer agreed, reluctantly – he agonised over the matter, and his attitude was that if that was the only way it must be taken because what was going on simply had to be stopped. 'Maybe I am going to sin in doing this,' he argued, 'but if so, at least there is forgiveness for sin'. That was how he went into the plot, and in fact he actually asked the Church not to pray for him, because he felt that he had no right to this when he was acting as a double agent, with a Nazi passport and all the freedom of movement it conferred.

He was arrested in 1943 before the assassination plot really got under way, and in prison he was able to keep in touch with the outside world surprisingly well; he did not have a tough time – it was a marvellous opportunity for study, however painful it was not to have his freedom. When his Uncle Rudi, a military governor, came to visit him they even had a glass of champagne together. He had the opportunity to write, and then it was that he realised how his church had failed his country. The most important of his writings for us today are those that criticise the Church and set out how we are entering into a phase of human existence that is completely new.

As the Americans advanced in April 1945, Bonhoeffer was moved from prison to prison. Finally at Flossenberg he was tried, condemned and hanged. Bonhoeffer was by discipline a theologian. In different times he would not have strayed outside the academic world yet his broadcasts and later his writings carried his beliefs for beyond a theological elite.

As the shadow of world war slowly and painfully receded, Christian protest and reform gradually became aware of the challenge of mass communication. If the people would not come to the pulpit, then the pulpit would have to be dismantled and taken wherever it was needed. Clerical in-fighting was unlikely to engage minds which had been through the horrors of war. There were larger, simpler questions to be answered.

C. S. Lewis, having converted to Christianity before the war, used all his intellectual talents to argue for his new-found faith. He was a born communicator and his radio broadcasts were immensely popular. He spoke about God but without a hint of churchiness. The clerical strangle-hold on theology was beginning to break down. Brian Sibley argues that although Lewis was an uncommon man he had at heart the questionings of the common man. On one occasion, à propos the question of pain, he said, 'If there's a God, and that God is good, then He must want to see His creatures happy. If He is Almighty and has got all power, then He must have it within His power to make His creatures happy. So you look around the world and you see that His creatures are not happy. So this means either that God doesn't have any power or He's not good or there's something wrong here that we can't understand.' That is a question that all of us ask, questions which theologians have been and are still frightened to ask. He was the man who was prepared to say, 'I don't understand that' in just the same way as you may say it of any non-religious question; and other people have responded to an extraordinary degree to the way in which he set about trying to find his answers.

Lewis had his failings. He could be bombastic and glib but he also challenged nominal Christians to face up to the limitations of their beliefs. He was no believer in deferential Christianity.

On the other side of the Atlantic a very different man but one with very similar motives was beginning a campaign which still continues today. In 1949 the son of a North Carolina farmer led a crusade for Christ in Los Angeles. His name was Billy Graham. His methods of mass evangelisation, calling on people to get up out of their seats, excited many and also alienated a few. Clive Calver admits that Billy Graham's manner – even his bright ties – made some people feel uncomfortable. Few have ever doubted the sincerity of his Gospel-based message, although there have been misgivings about Billy Graham's willingness to share a platform with anyone who claims to share his belief in the Bible.

Others reacted to the demands of the times in different ways. Roger Schultz, remembering his grandmother's reaction to the sufferings of the First World War, was determined to found a Christian community dedicated to making reconciliation a reality. He settled in a tiny village in Burgundy called Taizé.

Brother Emil says that at the beginning Brother Roger's vision was to try, with a small group of people, to live out a kind of parable of reconciliation, a parable of community. He thought there would be only a small number of brothers and that the first generation would not see any fruit for many years. But everything developed more quickly than he had expected.

The community is an ecumenical one, with brothers from different denominations, and from the beginning there was a conviction that

Christians could be credible only if they could give a sign of unity. That unity was never seen as an aim in itself, but as a kind of first step – Christians acting as a kind of leaven of reconciliation in the human family with all its divisions. The recruitment from different denominations was not a deliberate strategy; it just happened that things came about that way. What made Taizé different was the fact that Catholic and Protestant brothers worshipped side by side. It was and is an ecumenical community in fact, not one merely in aspiration.

Catholics and Protestants, still separated in many beliefs, were con-fronted by similar problems. Chief among them learning to live with the memory of the Holocaust and with individual memories of survivors like Rabbi Friedlander, who recalls, in November 1938, as a little boy, run-ning through the streets of Berlin to hide during the *Kristallnacht*, the pogrom when many of the synagogues were set on fire, or plundered and wrecked. His image is of his synagogue burning brightly and the church standing alongside it silent with nothing being said. There were a few churches in Germany with courageous pastors who stood up at the time of the *Kristallnacht* and said 'Houses of God are burning', but there were all too many who kept very quiet about it. It was not simply a question of a failure in the relationship between Christians and Jews – it was the wider question of a great failure of the Church to take a stand against tyranny and inhumanity, a failure from which the Church suffered, and has continued to suffer, both in Germany and outside.

Churches which had grown used to being proud had to face their own failure. Slowly the lesson was beginning to be learned that Christianity needed to listen as well as to teach.

After Charles de Foucauld's death in the small village of Tamanrasset in the centre of the Sahara, idealistic and practical men and women calling themselves the little brothers and little sisters of Jesus gathered them-selves in small communities dedicated to living the life of the poor without any privileges. They took the lowliest forms of available work and tried to follow Charles's insights, many of which still remain in advance of our time let alone his. Brother Ian speaks of how Charles became almost a chaplain to the Muslims he was living with; he evolved various forms of prayer that Muslims could say with him without com-promise and was often called upon to help them when they were sick or dying. He used to say that God would finally accept everyone – a new and paradoxical attitude in the Roman Catholic Church which is coming to be more widely felt: a desire not to impose one's own culture and religion any more than to hide it.

There were challenges from within the Christian community as well as from outside. The World Council of Churches had been placed on the ecclesiastical back burner during the war years but in 1948 it was formally inaugurated at a meeting in Amsterdam. It has been accused of spreading the theology of the lowest form of common denominator. Fair comment? Dr Pauline Webb points out that the basis of belief in the World Council is really a very simple and in some ways minimal one: belief in Christ as God and Saviour, in the Triune God, in the Holy Scriptures as bringing that threefold revelation to us. Also it insists on good relations with other Christians. Some have accused the inaugural meeting of 1948 of being too optimistic, but Dr Webb believes that is an unfair charge. She says the conference which took as its theme 'Man's Disorder and God's Design' was very conscious indeed of the devastation in Europe, and its primary emphasis was on reconstruction, and refugee relief in particular.

That common work for refugees played a great part in bringing the Churches together, and there was a sense that it was better to concentrate on the service that unites than the doctrines that divide – a great phrase that came out of the 1948 Amsterdam assembly. Another significant phrase was coined by the Englishwoman Kathleen Bliss, who said simply, 'We now intend to stay together.' The movement was conscious of the problems it faced, but there was a clearer optimistic note at the next assembly, in 1954 at Evanston in the United States, which had the theme 'Christ, the Hope of the World'. In the early 1950s there was a feeling that a new order was emerging, and that Churches were moving towards unity.

The World Council of Churches excited church activists but what about those who would never darken church thresholds? Part of Billy Graham's success has been based on his practice of meeting people in neutral non-religious territory – the advantage is mathematical as well as psychological. Clive Calver points out that there is a great advantage in preaching in a stadium in front of sixty thousand people – you would have to go to an awful lot of churches to reach the same number. Billy Graham's conviction is that there comes a time in a person's life when he or she needs to be challenged as to whether they are going to make a commitment to Christ or live just for themselves. That is a challenge that can be made very well in the context of a crusading mission. It has to be remembered, however, that the Graham technique is to follow the challenge up with integration into the local Christian community.

The first half of the century transformed the Christian churches. As never before, Christians were brought face to face with their own short-comings and the strengths of others – particularly the weak. Charles de Foucauld, the failure, challenged accepted ideas about the religious life and the faith of non-Christians. Pentecostalists dared to bring emotion into mainline Christianity. Prior Roger and the World Council of Churches proved that Christians of different traditions could worship together. C. S. Lewis insisted that common sense and intelligence were not incompatible with Christianity and Billy Graham began a campaign which still gathers strength today.

But let the last word be with the unlikely hero of the Second World War, the academic turned plotter – Dietrich Bonhoeffer whose courage and questioning still inspires Christians today. Edwin Robertson thinks it often seems ironic that when Bonhoeffer was in America he should have said, 'I cannot participate in the reconstruction of Germany after the war unless I am with its Christian people during the war.' He was right, but after the war he was also dead – and in spite of that, his influence was considerable. It influenced the way in which the German Church gathered together and, particularly under the leadership of Martin Niemoller, made their confession of guilt – a confession shared even by people who had resisted Hitler and been in concentration camps.

Such people did not say, 'We were innocent – it was all the fault of the rest of the Church': they persuaded the Church to come together in solidarity and say with them, 'We failed the German people in their hour of crisis.' One pastor who knew who the local Nazis had been said to them: 'Tell me, young men, where did we fail you?' This was very much Bonhoeffer's attitude, and the attitude of the Church: asking forgiveness of those whom it had not been able to teach how to face the real facts of evil.

What Bonhoeffer wrote in his last letters has since stirred not only the theological world but a wider world too. What he said came from his own experience and was quite astonishingly revolutionary. His message was that mankind develops through the centuries, and that with the coming of the Renaissance there was also the coming of a sense of the autonomy of man. And since then, we have been gradually growing out of religion, which is surely a temporary phase in the development of humanity. What God is about, and what Christ is about, is not religion, though religion may still be and has been an honourable way of communicating it; it is, Bonhoeffer says, about humanity and making humanity as God intended.

*Pope John XXIII, the caretaker pope who revolutionised his Church
and enabled the log jam of Roman Catholic reform to be broken*

CHAPTER IX

LICENCE AND LIBERATION

The tears of disgraced tele-evangelists, the anger of women demanding the right to ordination and the triumphant peal of Christmas church bells ringing out over former communist cities are all part of the rich emotional mix which have contributed to the extraordinary and unpredictable revolutions in Christian thought and behaviour packed into the last fifty years. It has been a time when almost every religious pre-supposition has been questioned. There have been many great teachers and theologians – Karl Barth, Paul Tillich, Karl Rahner and Jurgen Moltmann – but they are only part of the continuing saga of Christian reform since the Second World War. In the main the running has been made by others whose names will never appear in any religious history books: the poor in Latin America and elsewhere, who have made liberation theology a reality, the thousands who claim that charismatic spirit-led worship is the way ahead, and all those who suffered for their faith in the days of the cold war and religious persecution.

Call it coincidence or providence, our times have seen enough implausible twists in the story of Christian reform continually to wrong foot even the most assiduous religious observer. Time and again the 1960s announcement of the death of God, epitomising the seemingly inevitable secularisation of the world, has been proved premature. The largest body of Christian believers, the Roman Catholic Church, has seen its Church turned inside out. Elsewhere the outlandish has become unremarkable. The Free Churches have their women ministers and the Anglican communion generally has its women priests. In countries where the Bible was banned, there are now openly-run evangelical crusades. Christian sectarianism is no longer seen as a badge of loyalty but as a mark of pigheadedness and as the world becomes more sophisticated many are taking refuge in a religious faith so simple that it alarms as many as it attracts. Everything is still in the process of change – yesterday's liberal is today's establishment representative and traditionalists find themselves cast as protestors.

But let us begin with a short, fat, traditionally-minded Italian who, in 1958, became Pope in his old age and managed to inspire such affection that when he died, flags in Belfast – not the most papal of cities – flew at half mast. His name was Angelo Roncalli. He is remembered as John XXIII. At the time of his election any Vatican watcher worth his incense would have marked him down as a non-starter. Peter Hebblethwaite, journalist and biographer of John XXIII, points out that he was nearly seventy-seven years old, and an unexpected choice – even though those who voted for him thought he was just going to hold the fort and keep the See of Peter warm until Archbishop Montini (who was the natural candidate but not yet a cardinal) could take over. So he was really a transitional Pope – or that is what everybody said. Somebody advised him, 'All you need to do is not to do anything at all. Say the rosary, give a few pious little sermons, beatify the odd saint, but don't try and do anything big – you're too old for that.'

In fact, within two days of his election he knew already what he had to do – call the Second Vatican Council. Why? As the Cardinals who had elected him came to say goodbye to him they found him with a huge globe beside him, almost as big as he was. He was swivelling it round and round with Cardinal Gilroy and saying things like, 'There's Sydney down there. How am I supposed to know anything about Sydney? I don't know anything about it. Do you know Sydney? You've got to tell me about Sydney'.

Many things were not working well in the Roman Catholic Church, in particular the relations between the Roman Curia and the local churches throughout the world. It had become quite clear to him that one of the reasons for this was the fact that the local churches never came together, and the only way to start solving these problems was to bring them together, to talk about catching up with the modern world – what he called *aggiornamento*, 'bringing up to date'. That, it seems, was his primary motive.

There had in fact already been a project which few people knew about at the time and not many more today. In 1948 there had been a project for a council. It was to last for six weeks only and be a magnificent display of Catholic unity after the conflicts of the Second World War, and it was to condemn modern errors. There were a lot of them on the agenda – existentialism, something called pansexualism referring to the increase in sexual promiscuity, secularism – in those days sins always seemed to be 'isms' as far as the Roman Catholic Church was concerned. It became quite clear that the idea would be impossible – everyone wanted to add something to the agenda, so the idea was abandoned, but not lost sight of. Pope John XXIII, in the course of his rummages through the archives (he was an archivist by discipline) saw what a ghastly idea this had been and declared, 'My Council is going to be something different, unlike any other Council in the history of the Church, because it is not being called to condemn errors. It's not that we don't think there are any – but condemning errors is not the way to deal with them.' In his own traditional phrase, they needed, he said, 'not the rod of discipline, but the medicine of mercy'.

And John XXIII lost no time in his search for that medicine. Archbishop Derek Worlock of Liverpool, who first attended the council as a train-bearer, remembers the day the announcement was made, 25th January 1959. He had just returned to Archbishop's House in Westminster, London, where he was working at the time, when someone said, 'The press are on the phone – Pope John has done it again. He's called a Council!' The press were asking if he could explain to them what an Ecumenical Council was, and he had to admit to them, 'All I can really remember about the last Council, Vatican I, is that I was told it would never happen again.'

None the less, the preparations for the Council went ahead over the next three years until, largely due to the perseverance and insistence of the Pope himself, and all the Roman Catholic bishops in the world were eventually called together in the autumn of 1962. There had been various preparatory commissions and by the time the Council opened it was becoming evident that the stakes were much larger than some sort of discussion of Christian unity and a little general tidying up.

The really big issue to come under consideration was the relationship between the local church and Rome. On the opening day of the Council the Pope insisted that it must look at the teaching of the Church in order to try and make it intelligible in modern terms. It became clear that what was really being looked at was nothing less than the whole nature and mission of the Church.

The Vatican Council was to last for three years. Its decisions changed the religious life of Roman Catholics more than any other council in the history of that Church. The log jam of reform within the Catholic Church had been broken. Church services were rapidly modernised. Siege-mentality against other Christians or those of other faiths was no longer sanctioned. For many, like the rebel Archbishop Marcel Lefebrve, the reform went too far and too fast. In the years immediately after the Council Catholics saw their Church, once unchangeable, convulsed by change. Even now the shock waves of the Council are still being absorbed.

But the Vatican was not the only religious body to go through the furnace of controversy. In 1968 the twenty-year-old World Council of Churches was about to lose its innocuous image. Dr Pauline Webb says that the Assembly at Uppsala was a real turning point. It was in 1968, at the time of the student riots in Paris and an outburst of revolutionary zeal in general. Its theme was, significantly enough, 'Behold, I make all things new', and in a vivid image Dr Webb describes it as the Assembly at which the Churches, instead of standing round in a circle holding hands and looking inwards, turned round and started to look at the world outside them. The great cloud hanging over the Assembly was racism, and it has been said that the most eloquent speaker there was a voice that was never heard – Martin Luther King, who had been assassinated a few weeks before.

One of the most eloquent voices that *was* heard was that of the black American novelist James Baldwin, who really aroused the Assembly by saying that there had been enough of resolutions against racism; what was wanted was real action. The Uppsala Assembly was to launch a programme of action against racism which was to prove controversial out of all proportion to its modest size.

The heart of the action programme was money. A special fund was raised to give humanitarian aid to liberation movements struggling against racism not only in South Africa but all across the world. This of course created an enormous amount of controversy, because some of the movements concerned were engaged in armed struggle. There was furious debate about why the Council of Churches had done this, and, more importantly, about the nature of racism and about what it really meant to work together and take risks together.

In many countries of the Third World Christianity became inseparable from taking risks. Across the denominations Christian priests and lay workers began to realise that they could not preach the Gospel without attacking the oligarchies and dictatorships which institutionalised poverty.

This new – and really very old – theology was called Liberation Theology. Its starting points were not abstract ideas or principles but the hardship and injustice experienced by people struggling to live. It attacked secular structures and questioned ecclesiastical ones. In many places in Latin America the former rigidly pro-establishment Catholic hierarchy was turned on its head. Those in power were no longer import-ant – the Church belonged to the powerless. New forms of church organisation grew up to reflect that shift of emphasis – among them the 'basic communities'. Fr Michael Campbell-Johnston, Provincial of the British Jesuits, who has spent 25 years in the Third World, describes basic communities as being simply the Christians in a particular village or suburb who came together and said 'We want to worship God as a group, but we do not want to do it just in church. We belong to this society and we want to take a look at it, and see what needs to be changed to make it more just.' They deliberately tried to make themselves more aware of the injustices around them. A great Brazilian educator coined the 'conscienti-sation' to describe this process of making people aware of the injustice around them and the fact that they themselves needed to change it.

Take for example one of the sentences used to teach illiterate peasants in North-East Brazil how to write. Traditional sentences for teaching reading are things like 'The cat sat on the mat' and so on. Instead the liberation theologians used sentences like: 'John is a peasant. He works hard all day. His children are hungry. Why?' Simple enough, but dyna-mite. That is exactly the kind of effect the basic Christian communities have tried to achieve. They look at the situation, try to understand it, and then look at the Bible and see what the Church says and decide what to do. This is how Liberation Theology operates.

Of course church groups were not the only people thinking about liberation. The Women's Movement was shaking male bastions all over the world and at all levels of society. This had its effect on the churches. Within the Anglican community it galvanised already existing pressure for female participation in the ministry. Dr Diana McClatchey, a deacon in the Church of England and a long-time campaigner for women's ordination, thinks that there was a realisation after the War that very many able women who were also very committed churchwomen might well have produced a very strong group within the Church and within the ministry had they been given the opportunity. But it was not on the horizon. Certainly the ministry of deaconesses was going on and women were being accepted more readily to some extent because they had started working in slum parishes. Numbers slowly increased and from the 1960s more and more women were becoming deaconesses; the diaconate was losing its fuddy-duddy image, and there was more and more to do, and the general advance of woman in all sorts of spheres began to have its repercussions.

In the 1970s secularism seemed to be making all the idealogical running. The established churches had their backs against the materialist wall. But there was one exception – the charismatics with their spontaneous worship and claims of healing power. Unlike the American pentecostalists earlier in the century, charismatics were and are no separate denomination. Dr John Stott, one of the leading figures in evangelicalism and former rector of All Souls, Langham Place, London, says that the charismatics were and are simply people in the mainline Churches who hold pentecostal views – which means, to simplify a little, two particular things. Firstly, they believe that after conversion and baptism there is a second and subsequent experience which they call 'baptism with the Spirit' – often an overwhelming and emotional experience accompanied by what is described as 'speaking with tongues'. Secondly, they lay great emphasis in the gifts of the Spirit, not only speaking with tongues, but also healing and prophecy though some would claim that there are other gifts of the Spirit that are more important, such as the gift of teaching.

Praying in tongues can be a pleasant, melodious sound but is it really more? Is it a religious phenomenon worth taking seriously? Bishop David Pytches, a convinced charismatic, former Anglican bishop in Chile and now vicar of St Andrew's Church, Chorleywood, Hertfordshire, agrees that of course there is a great temptation to call it silly; for many years he did so himself. But such a reaction, he says, expresses, in his opinion, part of a mystery. There are some things in the New Testament that are very plain and clear, but we are dealing with God, and in the end, man is never going to comprehend God fully. So it can be argued that the Church's ministry, and our understanding of God, have to be transrational – not irrational, but beyond reason, because you cannot put God into a logical box. The traditional Churches have a sophisticated

Guatemalan Christians at prayer – in much of Latin America and South East Asia, Liberation Theology has forced the churches to rethink their traditional role and structure

Charismatics – daring to bring emotion and healing into church services

spirituality, and are often content to be that way. But many people trying to approach the Church today cannot relate to it – which is one of the reasons why ninety per cent of the population do not come to church. But, it is claimed, they *do* relate to the things that the Charismatics are doing and teaching. Traditional Christians have problems with charismatic ways, but the non-traditional outsider seems to delight in them.

Other outsiders have found charismatic fervour off-putting. It has not been all gain in Christian reform over the last two decades. Particularly in America hard-line fundamentalist groups became more strident, insisting that their brand of literalist Biblical interpretation held the key to the problems of a world teetering on the edge of nuclear conflict. Armageddon was eagerly awaited – a worrying trait in a pressure group whose national government has a formidable nuclear capacity.

Elsewhere the term 'fundamentalist' became a slur word, synonymous with 'bigot'. Many non-bigots and many evangelicals found they were being tarred with the fundamentalist brush. So let us set the record straight. What is the difference between evangelicals and fundamentalists? Dr John Stott considers them to be fundamentally different. A fundamentalist, he says, is somebody who is very suspicious of scholarship and science and intellectual endeavour in general. It would not be unfair to say that fundamentalism is an anti-intellectual movement, whereas the evangelical believes that all truth is God's truth, that there is no ultimate conflict between science and faith, and that one should be anxious to use the mind in the worship and service of God. The fundamentalist, on the other hand, has a very mechanical dictation theory of scriptural inspiration; much, in fact, as the Muslim thinks of the Koran as having been dictated in Arabic to Mohammed by Allah, so the fundamentalist thinks of the Bible as dictated by God. In contrast, the evangelical believes in what may be called the double authorship of Scripture, that it is both the Word of God and the words of men – the Word of God through the words of men. God allowed the human authors full control of their faculties and thought processes. Then there is the question of literalism: a fundamentalist believes that every word of the Bible is literally true, whereas an evangelical recognises that each book of the Bible should be interpreted in the light of its literary genre, and that there is a great deal of poetry, metaphor and symbol in the Bible so that not all of it by any means is intended to be understood literally. The intention of the author is really the key to how it should be interpreted.

A few years ago it seemed inevitable that the fundamentalists would have everything their own way. They saw themselves as the counterbalance to the so-called 'evil empire' of the Communist bloc. In the event, their faith in the strength of Communism has proved unfounded. The collapse of communism as well as the public and almost farcical disgrace of some of their best-known tele-evangelists has wrongfooted them.

Of course, many inside and outside the Churches have been surprised by the turn of events in Eastern Europe. Few foresaw a peaceful outcome to the Cold War. There were exceptions; among them, Peter Hebblethwaite believes, the Old Man of the Council, John XXIII. He was very much criticised for his attitude. In 1963 the Pope was quite close to death, and Khruschev wrote to him on his eightieth birthday – he had had quite good relations with Khruschev, considering the fact that papal relations with the Russian leadership had been nonexistent before. John XXIII had also sent a message to the Non-Aligned Conference in Belgrade, which was printed in *Pravda* – the first time a Pope had ever made its pages. He also intervened in the Cuban Missile Crisis, being the intermediary for some indirect communication between Kennedy and Khruschev which provided the latter with a way of climbing down without losing face. In the course of this he said that such a withdrawal would be an act of statesmanship and a good thing for humanity, and that he was sure Khruschev would be worthy of humanity. The next day a headline appeared in *Pravda*, 'Khruschev Worthy of Humanity' – a bit of a propaganda coup for Krushchev but still a lot better than a war.

Then there was the occasion when Khruschev's daughter and son-in-law came to Rome – which, technically speaking, was quite proper because the son-in-law was a journalist – and Pope John received him, and the Italian press was amazed and in many cases scandalised. Elections were coming up and people were saying that this was going to lose the Christian Democrats a million votes – there was a Church ban on voting Communist, yet here was the Pope talking to this Communist, so why could not he talk to the Italian Communists too? The Pope was well aware of all this, but his point was that if you continue appealing to the good that is in people then there is always hope for change.

Khruschev, Brezhnev, Andropov, Chernenko and Gorbachev have come and gone. The invincible orthodoxy of Soviet atheism is in tatters, but not before many Christian believers in the Soviet Union suffered untold hardships, persecution and even imprisonment for their faith. The

Soviet Union produced a remarkable vein of Christian protest – the still quiet protest of the spirit. For Canon Michael Bordeaux, Director of Keston College, the study centre for religion in Communist lands, one of the most interesting and exciting aspects of the development of the Christian faith in the old Soviet Union was the way in which spirituality deepened hand in hand with overt persecution. The spiritual life of the Church was never completely extinguished and in some places it burned very brightly indeed. It could not be fully seen in public but people knew how to find it if they really needed it.

Quite apart from the surviving monasteries there were even secret cells of monks and nuns in the Russian countryside, anchorites living in the depths of the forest as they do on Mount Athos, and people used to find their way to them and they continue to do so. These men and women were people of incredible spiritual authority. They were not part of any breakaway movement; they were part of the official Church. But they constituted a kind of subculture of the Church that was not really permitted, although everybody knew it existed. Such people had quite extraordinary influence, and Michael Bordeaux himself met a parish priest in Moscow who entirely depended on one of them. The priest, who was a very remarkable man in his own right, worked a twenty-hour day and when Bordeaux asked him how he, as an old man himself, managed to keep his faith alive and survive physically under such exhausting pressure, the priest explained that every six weeks he took a week off and went into the forest to talk to his spiritual father. He said, 'He directs me. He runs this parish from the depths of the woods. All I do is act as his spokesman, and listen to God.'

For all the progress in unity and spirituality in some parts of the world the injunction to 'see how these Christians love one another' still has a hollow ring. Is it too much to hope that one day the labels 'Catholic' and 'Protestant' may be forgotten? Archbishop Derek Worlock says labels are a matter of fashion. He was the only Roman Catholic in his prep school; he regarded himself as a Catholic and the others were regarded as Protestants. Later they became labelled as Anglo-Catholics, and himself as a Roman Catholic; then they became Catholics and he was Roman and he felt a bit pushed into a corner. He himself is perfectly happy to be simply a Catholic, and thinks that the actual bond of being a Christian is what is pre-eminent in people's minds. It is possible to be very proud to bear the designation of the Church to which we belong and also accept that it is not the case that everyone else is absolutely wrong – which is how Archbishop Worlock himself was, he says, brought up. That was a pure black-and-white attitude. But now Roman Catholics still hold their faith just as before but with the added realisation that many aspects of it are shared by others, and sometimes to an even greater degree. Labels should be used as means of identifying theological tradition, not as offensive weapons.

And what about the World Council of Churches and its hopes of unity among the churches? Has it achieved tangible results in its forty year existence? Pauline Webb thinks that the World Council has developed differently from the way in which it was conceived, widening its concerns and taking greater risks, and achieving much because of that. It has put anti-racism well and truly on the agenda of the Churches as part of the test of Christian credibility, and has also become very concerned about the role of women in the Church. Many Churches do now ordain women to the priesthood, but quite apart from that the Council has also been much concerned about the representation of women in its own deliber-ations, and there are now far more women involved in the leadership and representation of the Churches generally. The issue of the ordination of women is of course now becoming one of the most divisive where the ecumenical movement is concerned, and it is likely that the arguments about this issue will be helped towards their resolution by the World Council.

The issue of women's ordination is unlikely to go away. For Dr Diana McClatchey, the importance of female ordination is as much a part of faith as of principle: it is inextricably part of her understanding of the good news which is Christianity, and which, from the very beginning, applied to women as well as to men. The Gospel teaches that women mattered, and were valued in the eyes of God, and were worth more than many sparrows. Once the revolutionary step of baptising women had been taken, then the door was open in the fullness of time for their emergence as full individuals.

However true it may be that it is a question of justice, or of the Church mobilising all its resources if it means business (particularly in the mission field), it is more basic than any of that – far from being a departure from the tradition of the Church, it is in the tradition of the Church from the very beginning. Though it will naturally have expressed itself in different ways in different times and places, in this interpretation the root of the matter is the revolutionary assertion that all individuals matter.

In many parts of the world revolutionary assertions and Christian faith go hand in hand. From the days of the earliest martyrs Christianity has been seen as unacceptably political by its opponents. In Latin America priests have been accused of being crypto-Marxists yet in communist states believers have been treated as an unwanted fifth column. Totalitarian regimes of any description seem to have an inbuilt distrust of Christians, as in the case of the Soviet bloc which has been more than justified by events. Michael Bordeaux says that to begin with he used to think that the way in which Communism whipped up hatred against Christianity was really quite artificial – something he experienced for himself when he was a student in the Soviet Union in the 1950s under the Khruschev regime. Seeing that hatred, he used to wonder why it should be so persistantly fostered when the power of the Church had been broken thirty or forty years before. Later he came to realise that there had been more to it than met the eye because the Communist leaders, perhaps with some perspicacity, saw that the Christian Church was a potential rival, even a potential political rival. And so indeed it turned out. The Communist leaders, he thinks, could see this long before he ever did; if you look back at the political revolutions of 1989 in Europe you find that in just about every instance the Christian Church played a role, sometimes overt, sometimes behind the scenes but no less important for that, in every movement leading to the overthrow of Communism.

The collapse of communism has taken most people, believers and non-believers, by surprise. Are there any other changes of ideology waiting in the wings? Peter Hebblethwaite recalls that one of the themes Pope John was fond of in the New Testament comes in the passages in Matthew and Mark which speak about the signs of the times. It is really originally about predicting the weather – like 'Red sky at night . . .'. Jesus says, you can read the signs in the sky but you can't read the signs of the times, that is, you don't know when the Spirit is among you, you don't recognise it. It is an essential task for the Christian – he or she is by definition a traditionalist but he or she must also be open to the signs of the times, open to the presence of the Spirit, not just in the Church and her institutions but in the people and movements and tendencies of the contemporary world.

Of course this does not mean that the Christian baptizes everything uncritically. Pope John gave three examples of signs of the times. They can be seen as his legacy because they were in his last encyclical. He identified three movements which characterised the latter part of the twentieth century. The first is the end of colonialism, the second is the change in the place of women in society, and the third is the self-emancipation of the working class. All these things, he said, were vehicles for the Spirit.

This is an extraordinarily liberating teaching for anyone who has been imprisoned in thinking that the Church has its doctrine and its main job is to keep on saying it again and again without adaptation. This is a combination of the deepest fidelity to the tradition of the Church and the Gospel with the utmost openness to the modern world.

These signs of the times cannot be conveniently confined to distant countries. Michael Campbell-Johnston thinks we are seeing a new type of Christianity which is relevant to problems faced in the contemporary world. Liberation Theology is important not only for Third World countries but also for countries like the United Kingdom and United States, because so many Third World problems have their origins among the wealthier Western countries. We have to realise we belong to one world and there will be no justice in Brazil or Mexico or El Salvador until there is equal justice in the international structures of society and institutions like the World Bank and the International Monetary Fund. The fact that many poor Third World countries owe debts to the West which have been paid, sometimes, three times over because of interest rates is the kind of crucial question which liberation theologians are concerned about and wealthier Christians should surely be concerned about too.

Charismatic Christians predict a renewal in spirituality. But does this mean we stand on the brink of a great loss? In this enthusiastic all-embracing reform will we lose tradition and beauty and be left watching spires and steeples tumble down to the twanging of guitars? Bishop David Pytches maintains that the Charismatics do not intend to knock anything down, but that some things may tumble down if there are not the people to sustain them. At the moment, he claims, the Church of England is losing three hundred members a week, and has been doing so for the last ten years. At the beginning of the century there were only 5,000 Christians identified with charismatic renewal, but today there are 372,500,000 and some calculate that by the end of the century there will be 500,000,000. That would mean a much stronger Church, but you cannot tell in advance what form it will take. It would also arouse tremendous opposition in people who felt threatened by it.

CHAPTER X

UNFINISHED BUSINESS

Welcome to the supermarket. This chapter will not set out to make a religion of consumerism but it will explore some of the likely developments within the Christian community as the twentieth century slips into the twenty-first. To do this it is necessary to grasp three essential facts: first, the one certainty is that protest for paradise will continue and Christianity as we know it will change; second, it is probable that we will see a growing tension between those who want to defend a rigidly defined faith and those who will pick and choose their religious ideas from a wide variety of sources, not all of them Judaeo-Christian; and third, it is likely that church structures, all church structures, will be influenced by social, demographic and political forces as much as by theology.

Increased communication and mobility means that the options of belief open to people will multiply. Freedom of choice and the weakness of fragmentation will walk hand in hand. The supermarket of religious ideas stocking ancient insights, overpriced rubbish, truth and lies is already making its presence felt in the developed world. But the pluralists will not have everything their own way – the new House Churches will make sure of that.

High in energy, low in tranquillity, the House Churches have a surprising success story to tell. Love them or loathe them, they have reached out to many brought up in a post-Christian society where the closest brush with theology comes either through the booming science fiction-cum-fantasy literature which draw unashamedly on religious ideas or the imagery of pop videos which play on vestigial religious sensibilities to shock and to titilate.

The House Churches are firmly planted in today's world. Their strength, they say, comes from their rejection of yesterday's liberalism.

So, would it be fair to call them reactionary? Gerald Coates, Elder of Cobham Fellowship House Church, Surrey, says that when the movement started twenty years ago there was indeed an element of reaction, reaction to the liberalism that was creeping into the Church, and he believes, has since flooded into it. Many in the House Church movement claim that this is one of the main reasons why one thousand people a week are leaving the Church and have done so for the past ten years (and it was double that rate, they say, in the 1970s). The big growth of the House Churches in the 1970s came from people transferring to them from historic churches. The reason for it, says Gerald Coates, was the kind of pseudo-intellectualism of the liberals, who seem to some to have emptied the Bible of any rhyme or reason or meaning at all, maintaining you have to be intellectual to understand the Bible. This means that Jesus himself and his early disciples would never have got into any of their churches at all, let alone into any positions of authority. Certainly, he says, we do need to think through radically what we are doing and use our minds but many Christians have made the mind and the intellect a kind of altar on which the whole of Christian service is placed; so that if you are emotional you are looked upon as being second class, whereas if you are intellectual you are considered first class. According to Gerald Coates, this is sheer lunacy: today, all over the world, in Africa, South America, China, Russia, Romania, it is amongst the non-intellectuals that the flame of Christ has burned brightest. If you had said to journalists thirty or forty years ago that this was what was going to happen they would have said you were mad; but this, he says, is what has actually occurred.

House Churches come in various shapes and forms. Some have links with more established churches but the majority are independent, dissatisfied with the lukewarmness of the historic churches. They meet in groups of anything from ten to a thousand, hiring halls for larger meetings and using people's homes for smaller ones. They reject traditional liturgical forms. There are leaders or elders but not priests and ministers. Their style of worship is enthusiastic and charismatic and their appeal is to the young. Peter Brierley, director of MARC Europe, an organisation which collates statistics on religious allegiance, says that it is the young people who by and large are joining the House Churches, and their love of music is part of the reason why House Churches have a preference for music rather than quietness. Growth in the House Church movement is among teenagers and people in their early twenties. If you go to the more

The House Church movement rejects both liberalism and traditionalism and sees itself as the vanguard of a new reformation

mainstream groups the growth taking place there is not so much from that age group, but more among people in their thirties and early forties, and there is also a gender difference. The Charismatics tend to appeal more to men whereas the more mainstream groups tend to appeal to families, men and women more or less equally. One can only guess at the reasons why men are attracted to the House Churches – it may be because of the authority they are given, or because they see people already in responsible positions there. One big question is whether the exuberant charismatic element will be carried on as the young people get older.

Of course it is not only within the House Churches that the Charismatics are a force to be reckoned with. The Pentecostalists who began as a distinct denomination at the turn of this century, and the growing number of Charismatics in every religious grouping from Baptists to Roman Catholics are bringing new freer ways of worship to the older churches. But is all this change for the better? Would the carpenter from Nazareth who calmed the storm and prayed for forty solitary days and nights in the Judaean wilderness feel at home among all the cheerful noise of these new Christians. James Dunn argues that Jesus had quite a few strong words to say about those who thought they were wise and despised the naive and childlike, and there is in the best of Pentecostal worship an element of that kind which, he thinks, Jesus would have been drawn to.

The House Church and Charismatic or Pentecostalist revival is a worldwide phenomenon. It is part of a more general movement away from monolithic religious organisation to more local-based groups. This has particularly affected the churches of Africa. Dr Gordon Ossei Mensah, itinerant preacher with the Billy Graham Association, agrees there is a certain amount of fragmentation, though not as much today as in the 1960s and 1970s. He has a feeling that this earlier phenomenon was really a result of the independence that came to the African countries – all of a sudden people felt a freedom to do their own thing, and if they did not agree with the leadership of the particular church they belonged to they withdrew, and set up their own prayer house, which became a church in turn. If there was a dispute the tendency was, instead of settling it, to withdraw and set up on your own. There were other reasons. For example, some people might have gifts of healing and would be told that in the tradition of their church such things were not allowed – a healing ministry must come from the ordained pastor. So again, if people found that they had no chance to exercise gifts God had given them for the benefit of the whole congregation, they would, again, withdraw and set up their own church and place of healing. All these factors were reasons for fragmentation.

Nowhere are the claims made for the new style churches greater than in China. Naturally enough, the lack of structure of the House Church movement lends itself particularly well to a country where Christianity still carries with it the all-pervading threat of government disapproval. You will hear claims that Chinese House Churches have adherents running to millions. That may or may not be true – any sort of statistic coming out of China is likely to be unreliable. And there is another factor to take into account – the very independence of the House Church Movement makes it highly attractive to those who want to practice native rural Chinese superstitions which are even less liked by the government than Christianity.

The Rev. Bob White, author of a history of the Chinese Church and chairman of 'The Friends of the Church in China', says that popular religion is, if anything, growing fastest of all in the villages, and it is something the Government very much dislikes. There are reports that there are groups who are really practising what the Chinese Government would call popular superstitions, who register as Christian groups and are then able to do it legally under this cover. And there are other groups which are merging Christian and Buddhist ideas and traditional Chinese popular beliefs – a tremendous upsurge of activity and ideas, a real ferment, but very much uncontrolled. Some of the numbers being bandied about in the West with reference to Christians in China are probably wild exaggerations, with more than a little wish fulfilment in them, but there had undoubtedly been very significant growth, certainly among young people. In the cities, post-Tiananmen, many more students and other young people are actually going into churches, and it seems likely that they are searching for a value system different from what they have known in recent years.

Christians of all persuasions in China have suffered in recent years, feeling the brunt of the cultural revolution. Since then their fortunes have waxed and waned in tune with government paranoia. At the moment ground gained in the late 1980s has been lost but there is no doubt that Chinese Christianity will survive.

One of the oddities of Christian history is that long-run persecution seems to strengthen the churches. Is it then fair to say that persecution is good for the Church? Canon Michael Bordeaux thinks it is and it is not. He says it is undoubtedly true that spirituality deepens under persecution, just as it did in New Testament times. The doctrines of the Christian Church emerged in the third century under heavy persecution, and without that Roman persecution we should not have had the Creeds and the great Fathers of the Church, at least in the form in which we do have them. But if you look at the areas of Eastern Europe which have recently overthrown communism you can see that everywhere the institutions of the Church have been devastated. It will take fifty years to rebuild theological education in Czechoslovakia, or Hungary, or Romania; the institutions of the Church have been so heavily hit that they simply cannot pull themselves up by their own boot-straps. They desperately need help from the West in terms of printed books and seminary teachers. It is little use to open the doors of a new seminary if you have no teachers inside – and here there has been no theological education for generations. These are major problems of reconstruction.

Yet it is interesting to think whether, if there had not been persecution of the Russian Orthodox Church from 1917 onwards (which was the worst example), should we now be looking at a weaker or stronger Russian Orthodox Church? It probably has fifty million members after those years of persecution, and it may well be that the Russian Orthodox Church might well be less strong if there had been no persecution at all.

And freedom from one sort of totalitarianism brings its own dangers. Having shed communism, eastern Europe is not only fascinated by the glitter of consumerism but is also flirting with the cults which have grown up in the West over the last two decades. As in the West, young people in the former Soviet bloc will drift in and out of the cults but this is not the most important cultic challenge facing the churches according to Dr Eileen Barker, a sociologist of religion at the London School of Economics. She says that the cultic milieu is more of a challenge to the churches than particular cults. A sign of this cultic milieu is the wide variety of non-Christian ideas floating round, for instance reincarnation. About a quarter of the British population believes in reincarnation and many of them also believe in the resurrection without seeing any incompatibility between the two ideas. There are also a large number of eastern ideas, psycho-analytical theory and self-development teachings which are all tied up in finding the 'god within'. Even mainline Christians are affected by non-Judaeo-Christian or cultic ideas.

The religious supermarket is more likely to dilute Christian thought than the cultic corner shop. In Western Europe church-going may be declining but that is not necessarily an accurate index of disbelief. Peter Brierley says that an interesting finding which has emerged in a recent English church census is that the number of people who would call themselves Christians has not actually changed in the last ten years. About 47 per cent of the population will still say that they are Christian, but they do not go to church on a regular basis although they believe in God. If they go into hospital and are asked for their religion they say 'C of E' or 'Methodist' or 'R.C.' and that figure has not actually changed, so there is evidently a residual religiousness or religiosity or God-consciousness, call it what you will, which is still there and it is a Christian God-consciousness. Peter Brierley does not see this disappearing, at least not quickly: in a millennium, perhaps, but not in a century, let alone a decade.

For the House Churches a vague God-consciousness is not enough. Is it true to see them as the Reformation of the late twentieth century? Gerald Coates would like to think so. He believes that the people of Britain do deserve a strong faith in Christ and a strong faith in individual and corporate morality. The House Churches, he says, are not interested in American fundamentalism with its narrow-minded bigotry and inability to communicate in dialogue with people of other persuasions or indeed other faiths. But they do believe that there needs to be a very strong moral lead given to the country.

The roots of the House Church movement are conservative and evangelical, and although the media always tend to concentrate on the conservatism, says Gerald Coates, it is the style and form which are so different. Most of the House Churches believe in what may be called a non-religious approach to Christianity – no more special buildings, holy buildings, holy days, holy clothes, holy people. Only God is holy – and his people. The vastly greater part of growth in the House Churches now is through people who have no church background and no understanding of the Bible – they have, literally, grown up at home without the Bible ever being opened and they are intrigued by this new approach to Christianity.

But what about the more traditional churches? The House Church Movement represents one type of reformation but it is not necessarily the only model. Orthodox Christianity is thriving and Roman Catholicism which still accounts for six out of every ten Christians looks set to be further changed by a third Vatican Council, held perhaps early in the third millenium. Hans Küng, Catholic priest and veteran protestor, has some ideas for its agenda. He says the Catholic Church should sanction intercommunion at the local level, so that Catholics could go to Anglican or Protestant services and Anglicans would be welcome in the Catholic Eucharist. This would be a great step forward, and progress could then be made along the lines of Vatican II to settle questions like birth control, the ordination of women and, particularly, the equal rights of women in the Roman Catholic Church.

The Roman Catholic Church is not the only church which has had to listen to women campaigning for female ordination. The Rev Betty Bone-Sheiss, one of the Philadelphia Eleven, the first women to be ordained in the American Episcopal Church, believes that the churches could not stand aloof from secular campaigns for female equality. To act in a way that was discriminatory, she says, diminished not only those women who seek ordination: to deny one woman ordination is to say to all women that they are the second order of creation. It was a matter of helping the Church to become fully credible. Betty Bone-Sheiss loves to tell the story of how, after the Philadelphia Eleven gave communion to the two thousand people present at their ordination, an elderly woman stayed kneeling in front of the altar, and she went over to see if she could help her up. The woman was in floods of tears and said, 'No, no, I'm perfectly all right – but you know, this is the first time I knew it meant me.' If the Church could do that, Betty Bone-Sheiss maintains, for women who had felt left out of Christ's redemptive acts, but chose not to do it, then it was missing a great opportunity to do good. Not to ordain women said something to all women about their second order status in God's creation; and that, she says, was somehow heretical.

It is worth remembering that the first woman priest of the Anglican communion was Florence Li Tim Oi. There is a constant temptation to discount the contribution to Christian life coming from the one in five of the world's population – the Chinese. The religious supermarkets of the West may stock plenty of non-Christian eastern ideas but there are now signs that Christianity is beginning to take its place among the ideological influences on non-Christian Chinese. Bob White of The Friends of the Church in China makes the point that some intellectuals in China who

Florence Li, the first Anglican woman priest, greeting the newly consecrated Bishop Barbara Harris

come from a non-Christian background and are not members of the Church have none the less become increasingly interested in Christianity. There has actually been a new journal published called *The Christian Cultural Review*, which is produced by academics who are not for the most part Christians themselves, although one or two of them have said that they are coming to accept Christianity through their studies. For the first time in this century, maybe, there is a significant number of highly educated Chinese who are interested in religious questions, and one reason for this is that within the Western tradition they find that the individual is valued, which is important to them in terms of human rights.

Chinese tradition itself does not have the same emphasis, and these people feel that the Western approach comes from the Christian emphasis on the individual; and China, they feel, has has desperate need of it – something which they feel all the more strongly since Tiananmen although they cannot say this publicly. Christianity is very much relevant for them – and this intellectual ferment going on in academic circles in China is perhaps more important than the rather fundamentalist style of Christianity which can be found in many villages but could so easily become not much more than a kind of religious ghetto. Many young Chinese will go to church but will not actually join it – it is not untypical for them to say that they never want to join the Church, all the more so if they are pressed to join. This is because they and their parents were forced to join so many things in the Cultural Revolution that they never want to join any organisation ever again.

In one form or another Christian influence is growing in China. Liberation theology and the charismatic movement are bringing the churches of South America alive and in Africa there is growth across the denominational board. According to Dr Ossei Mensah, African Christianity is unstoppable provided it is accompanied by training for leadership, but he says if the leadership becomes overwhelmed by the influx of new believers and newcomers are not properly looked after and given a Christian training, then the growth will die out, because people simply will not wait around indefinitely on the fringe of the Church. If their interests are not being responded to they will look somewhere else, and of course Islam is a very great rival, not to mention many other religious bodies that will try to fill the gap.

The Church of the twenty-first century will belong more to the southern than the northern hemisphere. Inevitably it will be the Church of the poor. Professor James Dunn believes it will also become predominantly Pentecostal. He points out that Pentecostalism, which began in quite a small way in the southern states of America, has grown quite rapidly, particularly in Latin America and Africa – so much so that by far and away the most extensive non-Catholic Churches in Latin America are Pentecostal. In Africa a lot of the independent Churches which reacted against the old missionary-established Churches and their imported European traditions are Pentecostal in character, and the same holds good in South-East Asia and Indonesia. Given the decline of Christianity in the West it may well be that by the year 2000 Pentecostalism will be the dominant form of Christianity in the world.

Christianity looks as if it is about to be pulled in two different directions. One groundswell of energy seems to be pulling it towards a simple undiluted celebration of faith and other forces seem to be moving towards a more complex religious landscape which is rich in exotic and not necessarily Christian ideas. As Dr Eileen Barker again puts it, there is no longer a single 'sacred canopy' of religious ideas with clearly defined boundaries.

On the one hand you get, because of this, the New Age package of loose ideas which are tied up with the idea of the feminine, the Green theme of responsibility for the planet, the yin-yang balance, the importance of the individual and the self, and so on. At the other extreme you get the growth of fundamentalism in Islam, Christianity and even Hinduism (which you might have thought was a contradiction in terms). Then there is the general interaction between the effort to come together in ecumenical movements and the schismatic movements of trying to get back to religious purity – a vast flow and interweaving of ideas and values, in which the great themes of freedom, equality, justice and the rest take on the new rhetoric of new ideologies.

But surely after two thousand years of Christian thought there must be something better on the horizon than acceptance of every vague religious notion on the one hand and over-simple fundamentalism on the other? Can we take it for granted that Christianity will survive or is there a question mark over its very continuation? Hans Küng thinks that there is a great question mark because we are entering a new epoch of world history. We have a chance to establish a new global order; there are many forces ranged against that endeavour, and the problems are tremendous, but there are also many people all over the world who want to commit themselves to that new world ethic and new world order. It is to be hoped that the politicians will realise that the question mark is not only for the Churches. One great function the Churches could have in this situation is a prophetic function – speaking out about all these matters; not just criticising the politicians, but pointing to what would be the more positive possibilities.

And there is always the unexpected. No one would have predicted the collapse of Communism in the late 1980s and early 1990s. Michael Bordeaux believes it may have unforeseen repercussions, and that in the rush towards modernism of all sorts within the Church something has been lost – an adherence to very strictly traditional values, not simply in worship but also in morals, the great doctrines of the New Testament and the Creeds. Churches in the ex-Communist doctrines do, it seems, stick much more closely to such doctrines than many in the West, and the reason is clear: they have been beleaguered, a fortress of morality against the immorality of the Communist system. Obviously, that situation changes once the power of Communism in a country has been broken, but it has made a contribution to the traditional values of the Christian faith in a time when, in other parts of the world, those values have been to a great extent challenged.

It seems unlikely that in the world we live in with its highly developed international communications that the faithful restatement of those values will go unnoticed. In the amalgam that comes out of all this in the twenty-first century, some of these considerable portions of Christian mankind – the strong Churches in Poland and in Russia, for instance – will have much to contribute: modernism will not have it all its own way, and something of what has happened in such countries will be preserved.

So the twenty-first century beckons Christianity down several paths: tradition rediscovered, faith strengthened or weakened by insights from other beliefs or new expressions of certainty. The final outcome will depend on the protestors who will speak out in and for the next century. For as long as Christianity is alive, it will be more threatened by ease than hardship and will never be able to take success for granted. As Peter Brierley says: 'Christianity at heart is about a Cross. A cross is uncomfortable, it talks of sacrifice. When you're surrounded by plenty, talk of sacrifice often falls on deaf ears, therefore it is easy to take up some of the advantages of Christianity but not necessarily to follow through to the bitter end.'

*The Festival of Mind, Body and Spirit, part of the New Age
Movement, a tantalising mixture of insight and rubbish*

CONTRIBUTORS

Marilyn Adams, Professor of Philosophy, University of California

Olive Anderson, Professor of History, Queen Mary and Westfield College, London University

Cornelius Augustijn, Professor of History, Amsterdam University

Dr Eileen Barker, Sociologist of Religion, London School of Economics.

Fran Beckett, The Shaftesbury Society

Dom Aidan Bellenger OSB, Headmaster, Downside School

Dr Bob Bliss, Lecturer in American History, Lancaster University

The Rev Betty Bone-Sheiss, American Episcopal Church

Canon Michael Bordeaux, Director of Keston College

John Bossy, Professor of History, York University

Shirley du Boulay, biographer of Teresa of Avila

Peter Brierley, Director of MARC Europe

Dr Susan Brigdon, Fellow of Lincoln College, Oxford University

John Briggs, Director of the Victorian Studies Centre, Keele University

Peter Burke, Fellow of Emmanuel College, Cambridge University

General Eva Burroughs, Leader of The Salvation Army

Clive Calver, Director of the Evangelical Alliance

Fr Michael Campbell-Johnston SJ, Provincial of the British Jesuits

Gerald Coates, Elder of the Cobham Fellowship House Church, Surrey

Patrick Collinson, Regius Professor of Modern History and Fellow of Trinity College, Cambridge

Dr Peter Cotterell, Principal of the London Bible College

Clare Cross, Professor of History, York University

Dr Eamon Duffy, Magdalene College, Cambridge University

Alistair Duke, Senior Lecturer in History, Southampton University

James Dunn, former Professor of New Testament Studies, Durham University

Brother Emil, Member of the Taizé Community

Fr Philip Endean SJ, Campion Hall, Oxford

Dr Donald English, former President of the Methodist Conference of Great Britain

Rabbi Albert Friedlander, Leader of the Westminster Synagogue, London

Jonathan Fryer, biographer of George Fox

Bernard Hamilton, Professor of Crusading History, Nottingham University

Peter Hebblethwaite, journalist and John XXIII biographer

Christopher Hill, former Master of Balliol College, Oxford University

Brother Ian, little brother of Jesus and cleaner at Imperial College, London

Anthony Kenny, Warden of Rhodes House and Secretary of the Rhodes Trust, Oxford

Fr Ian Kerr, former chaplain at Oxford University

Dr Alan Kreider, Mennonite Church historian

Fr Hans Küng, theologian

Gordon Leff, Professor Emeritus, York University

Professor Richard Marius, Head of the Expository Writing Program, Harvard, USA

Dr Diarmaid MacCulloch, Wesley Collage, Bristol

Michael and Andrew Mason, typists praestantes

Dr Diana McClatchey, Deacon of the Church of England

Rev Dr Alistair McGrath, Lecturer in Church History, Wycliff Hall, Oxford

Elsie McKee, Professor of History, Princeton, New Jersey, USA

Dr Gordon Ossei Mensah, itinerant preacher, The Billy Graham Association

Dr James Moore, Lecturer in the History of Science, The Open University

Dr Patricia Morrison, Art Critic of the Financial Times

Fr Robert Murray SJ, Senior Research Fellow, Heythrop College, London University

Bishop David Pytches, former Anglican bishop in Chile

The Rev Henry Rack, biographer of Wesley and Bishop Fraser Senior Lecturer in Ecclesiastical History, Manchester University

The Rev Edwin Robertson, biographer of Bonhoeffer

Fr Geoffrey Rowell, Chaplain, Fellow and Tutor, Keble College, Oxford

Jack Scarisbrick, Professor of History, Warwick University

Dr Bob Scribner, British Academy Research Reader, Cambridge University

Brian Sibley, dramatist and broadcaster

Dr Ian Siggins, Luther scholar

The Rev Michael Smith, Church Historian and Baptist Minister of Golcar, Yorkshire

Dr Brian Stanley, Tutor in Church History, Trinity College, Bristol

Dr John Stott, former Rector of All Souls, Langham Place, London

John Todd, Luther biographer and publisher

Michael Walsh, Librarian, Heythrop College, London University

Dr Pauline Webb, former Vice Moderator of the Central Committee of the World Council of Churches

The Rev Bob White, Chairman, The Friends of the Church in China

Archbishop Derek Worlock, Roman Catholic Archbishop of Liverpool

BBC Books would like to thank the following for providing photographs, and for permission to reproduce copyright material. While every effort has been made to trace and acknowledge all copyright holders, we would like to apologise should there have been any errors or omissions.

Page 8, 24 and 52 Ancient Art and Architecture Collection; 15, 19, 57, 87, 91 and 95 The Mansell Collection; 31, 82, 112, and 125, Marlborough Photo library; 39, 68 and 73, Jean-Loup Charmet, 45 and 65 Mary Evans Picture Library; 96 National Portrait Gallery; 101 Victoria & Albert Museum; 111 The Wellcome Institute For The History of Medicine; 115 Popperfoto; 129 Camera Press; 132, 138 and 145 Topham Picture Source; 146 and 155 Geoff Howard; 161 The Anglican Communion; 165 New Life Promotions.

INDEX

Page numbers in *italic* refer to the illustrations

INDEX